THE
Worshiping
YOU

Prophetic and Practical
Insights into Worship

TOM INGLIS

DESTINY IMAGE™ EUROPE srl
Via Maiella, 1
66020 San Giovanni Teatino (Ch) - Italy

"Changing the world, one book at a time!"

This book and all other Destiny Image™ Europe books are available at Christian bookstores and distributors worldwide.

To order products, or for any other correspondence:

DESTINY IMAGE™ EUROPE srl
Via Acquacorrente, 6
65123 - Pescara - Italy
Tel. +39 085 4716623 - Fax: +39 085 9431270
E-mail: info@eurodestinyimage.com

Or reach us on the Internet: **www.eurodestinyimage.com**

ISBN: 978-88-89127-67-4
For Worldwide Distribution, Printed in the U.S.A.
1 2 3 4 5 6 7 8/13 12 11 10 09 08

Dedication

This book is dedicated to my wife Barbara, a gracious and precious gift from God and to my children Kirsty, David, Andrew, and Jessica, who are a constant blessing and inspiration to me.

This book is also dedicated to those at Sydney Life Church whom Barbara and I have had the privilege to serve as pastors. You are a wonderful, God-loving, faithful group of people, and we love you dearly.

I also want to dedicate this book to everyone who has encouraged and supported me through the years, as I have worked to take the message of worship to the nations. I am deeply grateful and look forward to working with you in the years that lie ahead.

Acknowledgment

My deepest appreciation to Peter Bennett who helped me with this book in between his business trips to Fiji and Australia. It would not have been the same without your valued editing skills and input.

Endorsements

The first time I heard Tom speak on the subject of worship, I was quite moved. I felt instantly that this man had been given a powerful insight from God on the subject of thanksgiving, praise, and worship as a lifestyle. Tom's Psalmody International School of Worship teaching has been greatly received at our church and has impacted many lives. This, in turn, has flowed through to our church services, where people are worshiping with more passion, intimacy, and understanding because of their relationship with God. This is not a book about music; it's about lifestyle. If you are looking to develop and align your life with the most powerful force in the universe, this is a must-read book!

Pastor Rob Scott
Victory Life Centre
Perth, Australia

The Worshiping You presents the 21st-century Church with prophetic and practical insights capable of igniting a long-awaited flow of God's glory and power into the Church. It invites all generations to embrace a vital truth that could bring Church and city transformations. Tom Inglis has once again displayed the passion of the Father's heart through this very important message. Catching the heartbeat of his heart will bring you into a greater understanding of what pleases the Father—a worshiping heart.

Pastor David McDonald
On the Edge Christian Centre
Toowoomba, Australia

Tom Inglis has written a book that is a prophetic voice to those who have ears to hear and eyes to see what the Spirit is saying to the Church. This book makes you reflect on the most vital aspect of our existence—the worship of God alone. I've known Tom for some years and have found him to be first and foremost a worshiper. He is a practitioner of that which he advocates and sets forth a divine imperative for those of us who read this book. That alone speaks more eloquently than the printed page and reinforces the truth offered to all as a prophetic pathway to seeing our dreams and visions come true. Putting into practice the truths Tom advocates will change your life for the good.

Dr. Kevin Dyson
President, New Covenant International University
Lake Worth, Florida, USA

Prophetic in nature, this awesome book reveals what God is doing in these times and helps to prepare the Church for what is to come. As you read, you will gain insight into God's purpose for worship and the power and transformation that will result not only in the Church but also in our communities. It's a life-changing book, a truly prophetic word for the nations.

Rev. Dr. Margaret Court, AO, MBE
Victory Life Centre
Perth, Australia

It is my privilege and honor to have known Pastor Tom and his family for more than 28 years, and I have personally been impacted with the prophetic and practical significance of God's call to draw near as a worshipper.

After receiving a special visitation, Tom has faithfully carried this vision of a lifestyle of worship to the nations. The many Schools of Worship established through Tom's ministry on at least five continents have significantly helped equip the great end time army of worshippers.

The Worshipping You will not only bless leaders whose hearts are set on equipping the saints but also anyone who hears and responds to God's call to come up higher into His abiding presence.

I know that as you read, study, meditate and act on these revelations, you will warm the Father's heart and begin to enjoy a deeper level of meaningful intimacy through thanksgiving, praise, and worship.

Tom not only delves into the original languages in a easy-to-read manner, but the thought-provoking and action-inspiring nuggets he shares will encourage you to explore and embrace the fullness of a worship relationship with your loving Savior.

Be enriched as you discover the value of *The Worshipping You*—a word from the heart of God for you in these times.

Dr. Ed Horak
Pastor/Author

Table of Contents

Part Two

Forewords

Inspired by a godly prophetic insight, Pastor Tom Inglis has faithfully carried a bold vision of the worshiping Church to believers around the globe for almost a quarter of a century. Hearts have been stirred by his unique ministry and life restored to the practice of worship in innumerable churches worldwide, as individuals have been awakened to the worship of our heavenly Father in spirit and in truth.

The Worshiping You shares in detail the prophetic foundations of this ministry and lays a future course for worship well beyond many commonly held perceptions of the purpose and place of worship in our Christian walk. As you step into *The Worshiping You* prepare for your current understanding of the subject to be challenged and changed. No matter how many other books you may have read on the subject, none will prepare you for the awakening, the journey, and the future of Kingdom worship like the insights revealed through the pages of this inspiring book.

At a time when the acquiescence of the Church to the ways of the world is increasingly evident, *The Worshiping You* is a timely reminder of God's perspective on worship. In His Kingdom, it must have an uncompromising place of prominence in the lifestyle of every Christian and the life of every church. The vision conveyed through the chapters of this book confronts personal practices and denominational traditions that have omitted or displaced the ultimate authority on worship—the Word of God. Amidst such challenges, though, the readers are encouraged time and again with messages of promise, hope, freedom, and fulfillment as they embrace a lifestyle of God-centered worship.

The heart responsive to the rich message shared in this book will be rewarded with a walk with our Creator that will be more exciting and more intimate than we could ever have imagined.

Peter R. Bennett
International Christian Business Development Adviser

At a recent concert, Bob Dylan sang "a church without the Holy Spirit is not a church at all." I would suggest that, similarly, a church without real worship is not a church at all. That begs the question: "How do you recognize a worshiping church, and from a personal perspective, how do you recognize a worshiper?"

Charismatic and traditional churches over the decades have developed a language and approach uniquely contemporary. There seems to be a linear mathematical relationship that they have evolved:

Praise + worship = music

At first glance, my response to the title *The Worshiping You* was that it did not relate to me, as I am not part of the music ministry. This is a mistake of the most significant magnitude—one that if left unattended and unexplored will most certainly limit the depth of my relationship with Christ.

I implore those of you who have taken the time to read this foreword, carefully read each page of this book as if your life depends on it. Next to your day of salvation, revelation of worship as more than a church or music appreciation activity but rather a continuous daily aspect of life is the key to the ultimate understanding of God's heart.

Depth, revelation, and a working practical knowledge of worship will draw the Spirit, personally and corporately, and unify the

Church/churches in a way that no other activity can. This is more important now than at any time in history. Welcome to a world of true worship.

Edmund Koza
Elder of Sydney Life Church

Preface

In 1984 I had a remarkable experience with God in my office during a time of studying His Word. Alone at my desk, I was suddenly aware of the overwhelming presence of God, and I started to record the impressions the Lord was giving me. The result was a page of inspiring prophecy regarding the future shape and nature of worship among God's people.

Since that time I have had the privilege to share this prophecy with thousands of people who have borne witness with it and encouraged me to share it with others.

Later, in 1997, over a period of several weeks, time was taken to expand and explain in detail the original prophecy. Since then God has allowed a decade to pass before prompting me to make known the full extent of this prophetic word through the writing of this book.

The prophetic can be very challenging and extremely encouraging. It forces us to make a choice between staying where we are in our journey with God and extending our faith with endless opportunities to follow the leading of His Spirit. As you read this book, you may become aware of adjustments required in your own life or church to accommodate the principles contained in this book.

This book paints an immense picture of Kingdom worship on the earth and the contribution it will make to the greatest revival in history. It moves beyond the informational to the transformational. We are on the cusp of a shift in our perspective on godly worship. This shift will be radical, but the results will be supernatural. As the precursor to a great outpouring of His Spirit, God will find the worshipers He is seeking.

Within these pages you'll discover insights on how to translate this truth into practical action in your own life, the local church, and society as a whole. I humbly submit the prophecy and teaching in this book to you for prayerful consideration. I hope they will encourage and strengthen you.

As a guide to the text, please note that the statements in quotation marks at the start of every chapter are extracts from the original prophecy of 1984. Paragraphs in quotation marks in the body of each chapter reveal the expanded prophecy.

Blessings
Tom Inglis

PART ONE

PROPHETIC INSIGHTS INTO WORSHIP

The Prophetic Insight

The Prophetic Word

In May of 1984, I was in my home study in Johannesburg, South Africa, when I was suddenly aware of the wonderful presence of the Lord. I felt led to write down impressions and thoughts in my heart that I knew were not of my own invention. During this time, I wrote the following words.

The Church

"A time is coming when the Church will not rest, day or night. Congregations will come together in shifts to worship God, simply because they want to. Their theme will be 'Holy, Holy, Holy.' All activities in the Body will give way to worship, and worship will be the central theme for all activities. Countless thousands will be swept into the churches day and night as congregations continually flow into the sanctuary to worship the Most High God. They will be swept in like falling leaves upon a swift flowing river. Sundays will no longer be known as *the* day of worship but *another* day of worship."

THE CONGREGATIONS

"Congregations will not be satisfied by hearing an occasional sermon on worship or reading books on the subject. They will place demands on leadership to teach them how to enter into praise and worship and live the word of praise and worship. Churches that refuse to praise in spirit and truth will empty overnight, and those that do worship will be filled to overflowing to the extent that congregants will stand outside on the church grounds and in the parking lots praising the Lord."

THE PASTORS

"Pastors will have to organize their church services to accommodate praise and worship as the Holy Spirit leads the way. As praise and worship goes forth, the Word of the Lord shall be clearer to the listeners than it has ever been before. Pastors and teachers will be amazed at the growth and maturity of the worshipers, and God will receive all the glory for it."

THE CHILDREN'S MINISTERS AND PASTORS

"Get ready for a new wave of worship from children whose understanding of the things of God will overtake many who are unprepared. Godly children will separate themselves to praise and worship their Heavenly Father. They will follow those who not only teach worship but practice it as well. These children will go forth as a worshiping army that will astound even their teachers. Don't ever discourage their worship or stop the flow. Encourage them as they stand before God and worship Him."

THE MUSICIANS

"Musicians will stand in line, totally submitted to pastors and music directors waiting for the opportunity to serve in the house of the Lord. Chief musicians will train them, and God will give those involved in music ministry the capacity to receive the equipping and anointing He intends for them. They will stand apart from sinful worldly music, and their lives will speak clearly of separation unto God."

The Schools of Praise and Worship

"Schools will be established specifically to set a standard for worship in the congregations. Psalmody schools will start all over the world to train the Body of Christ, psalmists, and worship leaders. These schools will flourish like flowers in the desert after the rain, where no man has planted and no man has watered but only God has prospered.

"The students from these schools will soon become the teachers and the original teachers will move on. There will be a continual movement throughout the world of holy men and women with an overwhelming desire and objective to exemplify praise and worship. The Most High God will identify their job description as *worshipers*, and they will have no need of anything the world can offer. They will be known by their love and loved by their knowing.

"These men and women will have a supernatural ability to work and travel, to uproot, adapt, and resettle, to move quickly and be highly efficient. They will bring glory and honor to the Most High God wherever they go and will never be glorified themselves.

"The servant's attitude of these men and women will touch even the ungodly, and they will become known as worshiping servants who are loved and highly respected. All this will be such a work of the Holy Spirit that no one will take any credit. Even the five-fold ministry will melt into the congregation as we all stand before God in adoration and awe."

CHAPTER I

The Power of Prophecy

This charge I commit to you, son Timothy, according to the prophecies previously made concerning you, that by them you may wage the good warfare (I Timothy 1:18).

Prophecy and prophetic ministry are important because they are associated with the plans and purposes of God. They reveal the heart of the Father for the Church today and prepare us for the Church of tomorrow.

The apostle Paul knew difficult circumstances facing the young Timothy and wrote, encouraging him to use the prophecies previously given to him to wage a good warfare.

Prophecy is powerful because it is divine guidance. It helps us wage an excellent warfare against the devil, whose plan is to stop us from fulfilling God's purpose for our lives and ultimately establishing His Kingdom on earth. Every prophetic word inherently carries power for its fulfillment when it is received and acted upon with faith.

About one-third of the Bible is made up of prophecy that God spoke through people before the events happened. It took men and women of faith who waged good warfare to bring them to fulfillment. Many have carried prophecies in their hearts that sadly have never come to pass because they did not know how to wage good warfare.

Many have been deceived into believing that because the prophecies were from God, they would not have to do anything except wait for them to come to pass—but the Bible teaches the opposite.

Waging good warfare involves reading the prophecies over and over, meditating on them, confessing them, and visualizing yourself walking in them. As this happens, you are literally forming strategies in the spirit realm for the prophecies to come to pass. The power of prophecy does not lie so much in what has been spoken as in the spiritual strategizing undertaken by the recipient to bring it to pass. Prophecy gives us direction concerning where we are headed, but not necessarily how we are to get there. We discover this as we spend time with God.

> [The Lord said] *"Call to Me, and I will answer you, and show you great and mighty things, which you do not know"* (Jeremiah 33:3)

In a place of fellowship, worship, and prayer, you are bringing back to God what He has spoken over your life. As He gets what He wants from you, that is, fellowship, you get what you need—the fulfillment of the prophetic ministry. Prophecy is also powerful because it reveals God's plan for the future given to us in the present. Prophecy gives us direction for the future so that we can be good stewards of our present. Prophecy is reality that exists in a different time frame—God's timetable of events waiting to be manifested by someone who believes and acts on them.

God tells us He has chosen to do nothing unless He first shares it with His prophets. (See Amos 3:7.)

> *The Revelation of Jesus Christ, which God gave Him to show His servants—things which must shortly take place. And He sent and signified it by His angel to His servant John, who bore witness to the word of God, and to the testimony of Jesus Christ, to all things that he saw. Blessed is he who reads and those who hear the words of this prophecy, and keep those things which are written in it; for the time is near* (Revelation 1:1-3).

God wants, and in a sense needs, the partnership of man to bring about His will on the earth. He knows the plans and purposes He has for our lives, but He wants us to know them also.

If we use prophecy to show us where we are headed, we will have the hope, courage, and faith to get there. Prophecy gives us hope to which we can attach our faith and act boldly regardless of what we see in the natural. We have insight into the unseen realm that prophecy has promised us.

> *The power of prophecy does not lie so much in what has been spoken but in the spiritual strategizing undertaken by the recipient to bring it to pass.*

God will never leave us unprepared for what He is about to do, because He has made a covenant with us that we will be partners with Him to fulfill His plans.

> *When He, the Spirit of truth, has come, He will guide you into all truth; for He will not speak on His own authority, but whatever He hears He will speak; and He will tell you things to come. He will glorify Me, for He will take of what is Mine and declare it to you* (John 16:13-14).

The Holy Spirit is urging us to hear and obey in these times like no other generation before us. He is raising up a Church of excellence that will be more glorious than any that previously existed. (See Haggai 2:9.) Churches that thirst for the things of God are open to the prophetic ministry and are making the necessary adjustments to accommodate the great outpouring of the Holy Spirit. The Spirit of prophecy is the Holy Spirit prophetically speaking God's timetable to the Church (see Revelation 19:10). He is emphasizing the urgency of the hour and the need to change to accommodate the current and future plans of God.

Prophecy is powerful because it reminds the devil of our present function as kings and priests on the earth with the responsibility and authority to execute our Father's purpose in the earth now and in the future. Every step in fulfilling prophecy also reminds the evil one of his impending judgment and eternal doom.

CHAPTER 2
Continual Worship

These are the singers, heads of the fathers' houses of the Levites, who lodged in the chambers, and were free from other duties; for they were employed in that work day and night (1 Chronicles 9:33).

> "A time is coming when the Church will not rest, day or night. Congregations will come together in shifts to worship God, simply because they want to."

In the time of King David and for some time afterward, worship was given to God continually. (See First Chronicles 16:37; Psalm 95:2; 100:2.) The worship ministry was highly organized into groups of musicians and singers who took shifts to minister before the Lord day and night. Worship was expressed 24 hours a day using musical instruments accompanied by joyful singing and thanksgiving as a response to God's presence in their midst.

> *If disaster comes upon us—sword, judgment, pestilence, or famine—we will stand before this temple and in Your presence (for Your name is in this temple), and cry out to You in our affliction, and You will hear and save (2 Chronicles 20:9).*

"We will soon see a return of continual worship on a large scale in local churches around the world, not as a result of organized 24-hour worship events, but as a response to His presence in our midst. Continual worship will become so prevalent that it will seem strange to think there was a time when we limited it to Sunday services and church buildings.

"Christians will consistently pursue the presence of God in their homes and churches. The testimony of His presence and power will draw unbelievers to the church. They will also be drawn because of the signs and wonders commonly associated with those who love Jesus."

> *These signs will follow those who believe: In My name they will cast out demons; they will speak with new tongues* (Mark 16:17).

"God's presence and healing power operating through the saints will draw the multitudes."

> [Jesus] *came down with them and stood on a level place with a crowd of His disciples and a great multitude of people from all Judea and Jerusalem, and from the seacoast of Tyre and Sidon, who came to hear Him and be healed of their diseases, as well as those who were tormented with unclean spirits. And they were healed. And the whole multitude sought to touch Him, for power went out from Him and healed them all* (Luke 6:17-19).

"There will be such a hunger and thirst for the presence of God that our church buildings and places of fellowship will not be able to contain those who desire to worship Him. Church as we know it today will take on a different format. Churches will have to remain open literally day and night to accommodate the worshipers, engaging congregations like no other church activity has done before. The praise and worship will be accompanied by prayer and spill out into the streets with signs and wonders as a demonstration of God's power and love for mankind. In fact, many of the weekly meetings and other activities we presently participate in will give way to worship and prayer meetings. All this will take place because believers will have such a strong desire to spend time in God's presence.

"The key partners of prayer and praise, worship and intimacy, reverence and godly fear, will be much more evident in our meetings, and we will grow in revelation knowledge of these activities.

"Prayer warriors will partner with worshipers in local churches and prepare the spiritual atmosphere for corporate gatherings. They will blanket our communities, towns, and cities with God's presence and evangelists will come forth like Lazarus from the grave. Even evangelists whose ministries are seemingly dead will arise with resurrection power. Like Elijah of old, they will walk in a place of supernatural accomplishments through the Word of God that they carry in their mouths. The enemy will not be able to contradict or resist them."

> *The woman said to Elijah, "Now by this I know that you are a man of God, and that the word of the Lord in your mouth is the truth"* (1 Kings 17:24).

> *I will give you a mouth and wisdom which all your adversaries will not be able to contradict or resist* (Luke 21:15).

"*All things are possible* will be the order of the day and nothing will be withheld from those who are sold out to God, to His presence, and to His Kingdom. The miraculous will be demonstrated in abundance to meet people's needs. The reverential fear of God mixed with exuberant joy and thanksgiving will dominate our meetings. Out of this will emerge wisdom operating through ordinary people such as has not been seen since the time of Solomon. The church will lead the way in many fields, and God's people will be sought out for their wisdom."

Chapter 3

God's Holiness

Holy, holy, holy, Lord God Almighty who was and is and is to come (Revelation 4:8).

"Their theme will be holy, holy, holy."

We are told that it is a Holy God who inhabits the praises of Israel or His people. "You are holy, enthroned in the praises of Israel" (Psalm 22:3). This Scripture associates God's holiness with praise and suggests that when we praise Him, He makes Himself at home. The Spirit of God lives in those who are born again (see First Corinthians 3:16), but it seems to be praise that makes Him feel comfortable in our temples of flesh.

The Hebrew word *inhabiting* carries the idea of living with someone as in a marriage. It also has the connotation of presiding as a judge. Praise invites God not only to inhabit our lives intimately as would a marriage partner but also to judge the way we live. There would be no merit in praise if it were only to tell God how much we love Him.

Praise doesn't change God, but it sure changes us. God already knows that He is awesome (see Psalm 66:3), but few of us seem to acknowledge just how remarkable we could become if we allowed God to make us more like Jesus. Praise helps us become like Him, being transformed into His image in His presence.

We all, with unveiled face, beholding as in a mirror the glory of the Lord, are being transformed into the same image from glory to glory, just as by the Spirit of the Lord (2 Corinthians 3:18).

This is why praise and worship should be a lifestyle and not just an act. In this way, it can be claimed that praise and worship together are possibly the most powerful, life-transforming activities in Christendom.

Holiness seems to be the defining element of God's character that best represents who He is. It captures the sum attributes of His character and distinctly separates Him from all others. Being consistently all that He says He is makes Him holy. His character is flawless, and He is eternally and infinitely holy whether or not we praise Him. Praise is our expression of wonder, awe, admiration, and gratitude for all that God is and all that He means to us. It is simply our response to His perfect, flawless nature. We are commanded to worship the Lord in the beauty of holiness.

Give unto the Lord the glory due to His name; worship the Lord in the beauty of holiness (Psalm 29:2).

As we gain knowledge of who He is (see Psalm 47:7), we will understand His holiness and respond accordingly with praise. The only reason we neglect praise is because we don't know God the way we should. True praise is not based upon music but upon knowledge—intimate knowledge of our Heavenly Father. Music is merely the vehicle through which we praise. We cannot worship a God we don't know, yet so many try and are disappointed when He seems so far away (and unmoved by their efforts). He is as close to us as our knowledge of Him. The following Scriptures confirm this.

Your words were found, and I ate them, and Your word was to me the joy and rejoicing of my heart (Jeremiah 15:16).

Your testimonies I have taken as a heritage forever, for they are the rejoicing of my heart (Psalm 119:111).

It is knowing God and His ways gained through time in His Word that makes us joyful and full of praise. The four living creatures in Revelation cried out "Holy, holy, holy, Lord God Almighty who was and is and is to come" (Revelation 4:8). They were worshiping what they were seeing and experiencing—a holy God. We also worship what we see, but unlike heavenly creatures, we can see God only by faith as we spend time in His Word, in prayer, and in worship.

The Old Testament saints associated holiness with consecration and separation. God dwelt in the Holy of Holies in the Tabernacle, a place only the high priest could enter and then only on special days with much caution. His presence made the place where He resided in the Tabernacle holy. Wherever God is present, the place is sanctified or made holy.

God's Holy Spirit inhabits us when we are born again, imparting His righteousness to us. This imparted righteousness gives us the right to be in His presence, but we are still commanded to be holy. (See First Peter 1:16.) We are not to avoid His holy work in our lives—work that separates us from the world and its values. The born-again experience opens the door to righteous living, which is where the power of God operates through us to establish His Kingdom.

"As the church becomes more intimate in worship to God, the revelation of His holiness and all the ramifications of it will profoundly affect the Church. As we become more aware of His holiness, we become more aware of our sinfulness and His grace that enables us to stand in His presence and worship Him. This will lead to times of repentance in our church meetings that will flow out of worship.

"A thorough cleansing will purge the Church of sin and iniquity and believers will start to walk in a place of righteous living that they have never before experienced. All this will be initiated through the presence of God in our midst, with an undeniable work of the Holy Spirit touching the hearts of men and women everywhere."

> Praise helps us become like Him, being transformed into His image in His presence. In this way, it can be claimed that praise and worship are possibly the most powerful, life-transforming activities in Christendom.

CHAPTER 4

Worship Takes Priority

The hour is coming, and now is, when the true worshipers will worship the Father in spirit and truth; for the Father is seeking such to worship Him (John 4:23).

"All activities in the Body will give way to worship, and worship will be the central theme for all activities."

"Every meeting and activity, whether on Sunday mornings or Friday night youth, will prioritize worship, because of the desire of His worshipers to be in His presence."

Throughout the Bible, the central theme is redemption and worship. From God's perspective, the ultimate for man is not just salvation but also worship. Salvation is the first step necessary to an eternity of worshiping God. Since the time of Adam's fall, God has been redeeming mankind, drawing him back into fellowship with Him and worship of Him.

As we study the Bible, we see that the ultimate activity and priority for us in eternity is worship. Most of us would agree with that, but many would find it difficult to position worship as a priority in the Church before Jesus returns. We understand the importance of evangelism and its necessity, but we have sadly neglected the importance of worship and the relationship between the two. There is no doubt that God's priority for the unsaved is salvation, and this will never change as long as there are sinners, but once they get saved the priority must be worship. To put it simply, God's priority for the world is evangelism but for the Church, it is worship.

> *The Son of Man has come to seek and to save that which was lost* (Luke 19:10).

The greatest evidence of a transformed life is worship. Anything less does not signify to the unsaved that we are different from them. Worship sets us apart in the spirit realm and testifies to who we are, what we believe, and who we trust.

> *I will praise You with my whole heart;*
> *Before the gods I will sing praises to You.*
> *I will worship toward Your holy temple,*
> *And praise Your name.*
> *For Your loving-kindness and Your truth;*
> *For You have magnified Your word above all Your name.*
> *In the day when I cried out, You answered me,*
> *And made me bold with strength in my soul*
> (Psalm 138:1-3).

To put it simply, God's priority for the world is evangelism but for the Church, it is worship.

The unchurched desperately need to see that we are in love with God by the way we worship Him. They also need to know that He is a living God who is touched by our weaknesses and needs. They will never be impressed by how hard we work for God, but they will be impressed by our love for Him since love never fails.

> *Love never fails. But whether there are prophecies, they will fail; whether there are tongues, they will cease; whether there is knowledge, it will vanish away* (1 Corinthians 13:8).

At times we've given the unchurched a picture of an exhausted, sometimes corrupt and immoral Church, so that they are suspicious of us and would rather take other spiritual options in a futile attempt to find God. Sadly they are turned off to God—not because of Him but because of us.

They are rightly confused about the sincerity of our relationship with God because we talk so much *about* Him, yet sacrifice so little *for* Him. This leads the unchurched to believe that they have as good a chance of earning a *type of salvation* as a result of their good works. Because we have not worshiped the way we should, we have not given the unchurched perspective on how great God is at changing lives that are yielded to Him. Evangelism through local churches will be far more effective in our communities when we prioritize and practice praise and worship.

The devil has deceived us into believing that the only important part of the church service is the preaching of the Word or the ministry time. Of course preaching and ministry are vital parts in the life of the church, but not at the expense of worship.

The church should be a place where first priority is given to worship with receiving ministry from Him following after. Unfortunately, though, the church has at times become a place of self-seekers rather than God-seekers. These individuals are only interested in God meeting their needs and do not come prepared to offer anything in return. Church indeed is the place where God will meet our needs, but that should not be the primary motivation for us to be there. We should want to go to worship Him and fellowship with other believers in an environment of love and caring. God wants to touch our lives, but He also wants to be touched with our worship.

This may be to a great degree the reason the unchurched are not attracted to the Church. The very thing the Church was designed to do (convert men and women to be worshipers) has fallen short of the mark, satisfied simply to convert the unbeliever to Christ. The Church has been focused on getting them to Heaven—and that's good—but most people want to know how God will help them through today and tomorrow and the next day. When they know the possibilities of a daily intimate relationship with God rooted in worship, it almost certainly change their perspective of the Church.

The fullest expression of salvation is worship. When the Church understands this and practices it, the world will soon discover that He died for them and He lives for them too.

CHAPTER 5

Massive Evangelization

They ate their food with gladness and simplicity of heart, praising God and having favor with all the people. And the Lord added to the church daily those who were being saved (Acts 2:46-47).

"Countless thousands will be swept into the churches day and night as congregations continually flow into the sanctuary to worship the Most High God."

As worship to God is given priority, there will be a greater boldness to witness because of the tangible reality of God's presence in our churches. Believers will declare the power of God operating in their lives, homes, and churches, and the unsaved will seek God because of the reality of the believers' testimonies.

"There will be little need for advertising and promotion of meetings because His presence will be enough to draw old and young, saved and unsaved. Special events aimed at drawing people to church will become almost obsolete, and the only churches that have them will be those where God's presence is not being experienced. The transforming power of His presence will become evident to millions of unsaved, and almost instantly, they will come under the convicting power of the Holy Spirit and run to churches where His presence is found. Church buildings will be far too small to accommodate the inflow of new converts and home meetings will abound. Entire towns and cities will have Christian meetings taking place in almost every street.

"The unsaved will be drawn to these home meetings in such great numbers that these meetings will soon become known as home churches, where the presence of God is experienced just as in the local churches. These home churches will be submitted to the Lordship of Christ and local church leadership. God will raise up teachers and pastors in these home churches, and the activities that take place in the local churches will be taking place in these home churches as well. There will be so many added to the Body of Christ that the size of a local church will be difficult to put into numbers. There will be such a powerful presence of God in communities that the churches will start to cooperate together to accommodate the enormous inflow of new converts and backsliders. In fact, pastors will start to help other pastors handle the great harvest. For the first time in the modern-day church, there will be a genuine preferring of one another in love, as those in church leadership get their focus off their own 'kingdoms' and back on the Kingdom of God.

"Those who have faithfully served the Lord as local church pastors for years without seeing much fruit will suddenly be honored by God as He starts to fill their churches with thirsty souls. They themselves will undergo such radical transformations in God's presence that their former ministries will hardly be recognizable. The promises that God gave many of these faithful pastors years previously will start to come to pass. The extent of the influx of souls into their churches will be a function of God's presence and their preparedness for revival and growth. Pastors will no longer care about the numbers game, but will only be interested in winning more converts to Christ. There will be a unity among leaders in communities as they work together to help each other receive the great harvest of souls. Revival will sweep across the nations and will affect everything in its path."

This wave of evangelism will be defined by an emphasis beyond salvation alone. It will reflect a fresh revelation among God's people that the eternal consequences of salvation are more than just escaping hell—they are to forever worship God.

Salvation takes a person out of the kingdom of darkness and places him or her in the Kingdom of God, but worship takes a person in the

Kingdom of God and places him or her in the intimate presence of God. We've only emphasized the first step. Evangelism through the eyes of man is seeing men and women come into the Kingdom, but evangelism through the eyes of God is seeing them enter a place where they are giving eternal worship to Him.

> *Evangelism through the eyes of God is seeing believers enter a place where they are giving eternal worship to Him.*

He has put a new song in my mouth—praise to our God; many will see it and fear, and will trust in the Lord (Psalm 40:3).

God sees salvation as a path to eternal fellowship and worship. The two outstanding priorities in the Bible are the worship of God and the witness to the world by the saints through preaching and living the Gospel.

Chapter 6

Preparing the Saints

He Himself gave some to be apostles, some prophets, some evangelists, and some pastors and teachers, for the equipping of the saints for the work of ministry, for the edifying of the body of Christ (Ephesians 4:11-12).

> "They will be swept in like falling leaves upon a swift-flowing river. Sundays will not be the day of worship, but just another day of worship."

"The presence of God in our midst will be like a river that flows with power, influencing towns, cities, and the countryside. God will start to multiply the numbers in our churches as people respond to invitations to receive Jesus as Lord. Daily additions to the church will be common. One of the greatest challenges for local churches will be the accommodation of such an inflow of converts. However, those who are in the flow of the Spirit will have anticipated this move of God and prepared for it. They will have trained up counsellors and teachers, children and youth ministers. There will be a quickening of anointed ministers to cope with the suddenness of God's hand.

"Christians will start to open up their homes as training and teaching centers under the supervision of the local church, because the church buildings will not be able to contain the many new converts who need to be nurtured. Many will need no formal theological training to be used by

God. They will sit for days, weeks, and months, *eating* God's Word and spending time in His presence. Miracles, signs, and wonders will follow their ministries because God has molded them in His presence.

"This move of God will get the Church active in ministry and Ephesians 4:11-12 will start to operate to prepare the saints for the work of the ministry. It will be obvious to all of us that the Lord has come in a powerful way, empowering and releasing us for Kingdom work."

God has appointed these in the church: first apostles, second prophets, third teachers, after that miracles, then gifts of healings, helps, administrations, varieties of tongues (1 Corinthians 12:28).

> Most denominations will lose their individual identities, being drawn closer together in one corporate Body of Christ.

"There will be such a desire to worship continually that church buildings will be as full of worshipers during the week as on Sundays. In fact, many will be encouraged to attend worship meetings during the week so that others can attend on Sunday. Sundays will hold a special place in the hearts of worshipers for biblical, historical, and practical reasons, but it will become less significant whether we worship on Sunday or another time. This will help in practical ways to accommodate worship and the explosive growth of the church. It will also challenge the traditional 'Sunday morning only' church to make way for the changes that the Holy Spirit is bringing about.

"Churches everywhere will be challenged to change their rigid systems of church meetings, and a freedom will be seen in many 'structured' denominations. Open repentance for religious traditional worship that has characterized many denominations will occur. As they submit to the Holy Ghost, most denominations will lose their individual identities, being drawn closer together in one corporate Body of Christ. Worship will be the chief ingredient of the work of the Holy Spirit in bringing this about and will have the necessary unifying influence to prepare the Church to receive the flood of new converts."

Believers were increasingly added to the Lord, multitudes of both men and women, so that they brought the sick out into the streets and laid them on beds and couches, that at least the shadow of Peter passing by might fall on some of them. Also a multitude gathered from the surrounding cities to Jerusalem, bringing sick people and those who were tormented by unclean spirits, and they were all healed (Acts 5:14-16).

"Worship and evangelism will be inseparable partners causing local churches to experience explosive growth in the times that are upon us."

What a glorious time to live and see God work in and through our lives!

CHAPTER 7

Worship Principles

My lips shall utter praise, for You teach me Your statutes (Psalm 119:171).

"Congregations will not be satisfied by hearing an occasional sermon on worship or reading books on the subject."

One of the most amazing facts of the Church is that she knows so little about worship, arguably *the* most important subject in the Bible. Many other areas of teaching have been emphasized, but praise and worship have been neglected, especially from the pulpit. Worship conferences have, for the most part, attracted only those musically inclined and have left a void in the biblical understanding of what worship is actually all about. This has resulted in worship becoming something of a musical warm-up before the preaching of God's Word and other activities that take place in the service.

This doesn't mean that we don't have to teach, preach, or evangelize. We need to do this with a greater fervor than ever before, but we need also to address the subject of worship. As evangelists we must preach the Gospel of salvation to the unsaved, but as pastors and teachers we must preach worship to the Church more than we have in the past.

We desperately need to reach the unsaved with the message of the Gospel, and we desperately need to reach the Church with the message of worship.

Although it may sound harsh, we cannot neglect the Church at the expense of the world. A weak Church cannot influence the world and our strength lies in our intimacy with God. It enables God to equip us to better evangelize the world with the most powerful witness that He is alive. It is difficult to deny the witness of those who have just been in close intimacy with Jesus.

> We desperately need to reach the unsaved with the message of the Gospel, and we desperately need to reach the Church with the message of worship.

When they saw the boldness of Peter and John, and perceived that they were uneducated and untrained men, they marvelled. And they realized that they had been with Jesus (Acts 4:13).

One question we need to ask is why there are so many Christians available for the mission fields, but so very few ever go. Could this be connected with our lack of worship? If we're not prepared to spend time with God ourselves in worship, how are we going to convince others on the mission field that they should get to know Him? Perhaps it has been the way we've preached our message to the unsaved. We have emphasized conversion as a one-time event that brings people to God—but have we shown these same people that conversion is the door through which they also gain access to the privilege of worshiping the Most High God for eternity?

Worship is not preached from the pulpit as often as it might be, given the significance God places upon it in the Bible. Consequently many of us have had little practical experience with the full context of worship, because we have not been instructed in it. Jesus said we must worship in Spirit and in truth (see John 4:23), so thank God that this is all changing, and we are beginning to understand the importance and absolute necessity of worship. We cannot praise without knowledge.

> Intimacy with God will better equip us to evangelize the world with the most powerful witness that He is alive.

God is the King of all the earth; sing praises with understanding (Psalm 47:7).

The word *understanding* means that someone has been instructed in such a way that it will bring good success. True praise is knowing what God's Word says about you and applying it by the kind of faith that results in good success. Another Scripture says that praise is the result of knowledge: "I will praise You with uprightness of heart, when I learn Your righteous judgments" (Psalm 119:7).

The understanding of worship has been so neglected that we have often substituted worship music for worship knowledge. Some are inclined to measure the merit of our worship by the skill of our musicians or how up-to-date our worship music happens to be. But true worship is a response to knowing God personally and intimately. Worship is a spiritual exercise from man's spirit to God's Spirit. It's a spiritual interaction from man to God and God to man. Music and singing may represent a vehicle or medium for this, but they are not the main event.

We know that God is love and that love never fails. Worship is our reaction to His love, but if we don't know His love there can be no worship. If our love relationship with God is frail, our worship will be as well.

Worship is also a response to His presence, but we have narrowly defined this as a response to Him in *corporate* worship. This is based on the Old Testament understanding of the people meeting with God at the place of worship where His presence resided in the Holy of Holies. Today God has come to reside within us and our worship is to be a response to His presence in our lives. We are now the priests, and we have the possibility of making praise and worship our lifestyle.

Although all believers are filled with God's Spirit, we each have a different revelation of the knowledge of His presence in our lives, and this is the basis of our worship. The future of worship in the Church is based on a revelation of a loving Heavenly Father. It is our only hope to worship *in truth.*

The fact that Jesus emphasised that we must worship in spirit and in truth suggests its necessity. It is a command, not a suggestion, just like His command to Nicodemus that he *must* be born again. "Do not marvel that I said to you, 'You must be born again'" (John 3:7). The Church has no choice but to worship in spirit and truth as Jesus commanded.

CHAPTER 8

Worshiping Churches

God is Spirit, and those who worship Him must worship in
spirit and truth (John 4:24).

"Congregations will place demands on leadership to
teach them how to enter into praise and worship and
live the word of praise and worship. Churches that refuse to praise in spirit and truth will empty overnight,
and those that do worship will be filled to overflowing
to the extent that congregants will stand outside on
the church grounds and in the parking lots praising
the Lord."

"The Holy Spirit will cause a hunger to worship like we have never
seen before as the Church lines herself up with the command of Jesus. It
will truly be a revival of worship flamed and fired up by the Spirit of
God Himself. Although there will always be flagship churches throughout the world that God uses to inspire and encourage us, no particular
churches will be chosen as prominent leaders in this end- time move of
God. It will be much more a general move of God springing up all over
the world in congregations both large and small.

"Congregations will call for greater opportunity to fully participate in worship of their God as the Holy Spirit makes this truth a clear priority for the Church. This groundswell of enthusiasm for worship will force church leaders to decide whether worship will be a priority in their own lives. Many will be released for the first time into a new dimension of ministry as they develop a lifestyle of worship.

"Humility will flood the Church, and leadership will cry out in open repentance asking God to forgive them for their lack of worship in the past. Pride, which has masked itself through good works and religious practice, will be exposed by worship."

You younger people, submit yourselves to your elders. Yes, all of you be submissive to one another, and be clothed with humility, for "God resists the proud, but gives grace to the humble" (1 Peter 5:5).

"There will be dramatic changes in the lifestyle of believers as they move to accommodate the presence of God and worship Him. Worshiping churches will start to see their pews fill on a nightly basis with people who have a burning desire to worship the Most High God. This will be such an exciting time for the Church, and especially for leadership, as the presence of God sweeps through in a most profound way. God's presence will be in religious churches, but it will be there to resist them. As much as worshiping churches will be blessed by His presence, those churches that refuse to worship will be met with His resistance in the form of a military-like strategy to bring them to a place of surrender.

> *There will be dramatic changes in the lifestyle of believers as they move to accommodate the presence of God and worship Him.*

"Those leaders who choose not to go with the prompting of the Holy Spirit will experience increasing frustration at the widening gap between them and those leaders who have made a way for Holy Spirit-led meetings. Many of their congregation will leave their churches in search of God's presence found in worshiping churches. It will become so obvious that where God is worshiped in spirit and truth is where His presence is found to heal, deliver those in captivity, and empower the Church to establish His Kingdom.

"Religious Christianity will be exposed by its lack of worship. The spirit of religion will attack the Church with a hatred that has not been seen previously in modern history. Worship will separate the Church from religion but at the same time will bring the true worshipers into unity like never before. Barrenness will overtake leadership who don't repent and accommodate the Holy Spirit's presence. Their churches will become as graveyards. It will be almost hard to believe that God will bring judgment so quickly. But He will."

We are to stop just talking about worship and do it, fervently and with our whole hearts. We are to stop just hearing the occasional sermon on worship or reading books on it (including this one), and embrace it, live it.

It is time to individually prioritize worship in our lives, to worship Him like never before. As we do we will release a river of His presence, flowing out of us, through the Church and beyond.

CHAPTER 9

Accommodate Change

The wind blows where it wishes, and you hear the sound of it, but cannot tell where it comes from and where it goes. So is everyone who is born of the Spirit (John 3:8).

"Pastors will have to organize their church services to accommodate praise and worship as the Holy Spirit leads the way."

The Church is longing for more of God. This is a wonderful thing, but it comes with a cost. The Church will have to become more flexible to accommodate the ministry of the Holy Spirit as He takes us into greater realms of His power and presence. We simply cannot continue the way we are and expect more of God. While God Himself remains ever the same, He uses change as a tool in our lives to promote growth and draw us closer to Him. This tells us that He has created us with the capacity to accommodate and live with change, even though there may be times when we prefer not to.

God's leaders are precious to Him. Without them there is not much He can do because He has graciously decided to work His plans and purposes through them. Flexibility, however, will be required of leadership to accommodate what God has planned for the Church in the times that lie ahead.

We could liken wineskins to our capacity to receive or reject the things of the Spirit in the times we live in.

No one puts a piece of unshrunk cloth on an old garment; for the patch pulls away from the garment, and the tear is made worse. Nor do they put new wine into old wineskins, or else the wineskins break, the wine is spilled, and the wineskins are ruined. But they put new wine into new wineskins, and both are preserved (Matthew 9:16-17).

Inflexibility, religious thinking, and fear of man are symbolic of old wineskins, whereas an openness to the Holy Spirit and His leading will always ensure that we have the capacity to "contain" the new thing He is doing in the earth.

Every old wineskin once was new and had the capacity to store fresh, new wine. The tragedy of old wineskins is that they become inflexible over time. It does not happen overnight, and no one really notices until it is time for the new wine.

In some instances throughout the Church world, the old wineskins have become so accustomed to the old wine that dependence on programs has progressively replaced dependence on God. We have held the Holy Spirit under house arrest in His own dwelling with controlled meetings that stifle the spontaneity of the Holy Spirit. Worship has become polished and performance-orientated at the expense of anointing. Man has subtly become the center of our attention, displacing God from His rightful position, and preaching has come to show greater sensitivity to man than God.

The standards of righteous living and obedience to God have been lowered so radically that truth now looks like a distortion. Many have become man-seekers rather than God-seekers. Godly standards have become strangers to the Church, and the Holy Spirit is seen to be an embarrassment in front of unbelievers. All this has chronically limited our passion for worship. Thank God this situation is now giving way to a powerful, refreshing change as many men and women of God, including myself, repent of their old ways and strive to hear what the Spirit is saying.

If worship is God's priority then we must recognize it as the Holy Spirit's priority as well. Effective church leaders will learn to accommodate what He is orchestrating in the church, accepting that many current practices and priorities must recede in deference to the Holy Spirit. Such change will not always be comfortable, but empowered by the Holy Spirit, there is no need for it to be difficult. The change necessary to accommodate the *new wine* will not feel awkward, but will be a welcome relief from the status quo.

In Matthew chapter nine, wine represents the Holy Spirit. The reference to *new wine* means that it has the same character and quality as the old wine but current in time. It is from the same vine, the same Holy Spirit, being poured out in a fresh way into vessels that will accommodate Him. (See Acts 2:16-18.) The Holy Spirit will not give of Himself where there is resistance to change or lack of passion for the things of God. He is highly selective and will pour Himself out only where His presence is welcome and where He is allowed to bring maximum results for the King and His Kingdom. The heart of man is where the old and new treasure (God's Word) is stored.

> [Jesus] *said to them, "Therefore every scribe instructed concerning the kingdom of heaven is like a householder who brings out of his treasure things new and old"* (Matthew 13:52).

God's Word is changeless, but His people are not. There is nothing more important than continuous transformation in the life of a believer, as we progressively become more like Jesus. We're created to change. The evidence of God's infinite love for us is His continual working in our lives completing the good work He has begun. (See Philippians 1:6.)

Throughout the Old Testament, God's people experienced times of desolation, and it always related to their disobedience and lack of worship. As the most powerfully transforming thing man can do, reformation and revival were always related to God's people returning to the worship of Jehovah. Every season of desolation will be transformed when we worship. Worship decimates staleness. It's impossible to worship God and not experience the fresh anointing of the Holy Spirit.

Worship is the answer for leaders who are weary, discouraged, or want to quit the ministry. In fact, worship is the key for all leaders who want to get and keep the freshness of God's presence and power in the Church. Worshiping disciples will be birthed through worshiping leaders.

The Body of Christ needs to be taught how to live the word of praise and worship, and leaders will have to exemplify worship to their people just as King David did. We see in the book of Psalms that King David was a prophet who foresaw the kind of praise that was earmarked for a generation yet to be created, or more accurately, recreated. This can only be referring to the New Testament Church. "This will be written for the generation to come, that a people yet to be created may praise the Lord" (Psalm 102:18).

King David instituted a radically different demonstration of praise than had ever been done previously. In spite of strong opposition from those who resisted change, he revolutionized worship in his time and gave us the foundation for worship in our time. Jesus did not add to David's revelation but said we should worship in spirit and truth, building on David's revelation.

> *The Body of Christ needs to be taught how to live the word of praise and worship, and leaders will have to exemplify worship to their people just as King David did.*

"It will soon become very apparent that the worship of any church will be a reflection of the worshiping heart of the leadership of that church. Great worshiping churches will be known to have worshiping leaders, who have *fathered* worshiping children. A generation of young people will flood the church where true *spiritual fathers* are found. God will raise up a generation like Joshua who will not depart from His presence.

"Worship constitutes change, and change will become the normal order. Our goal will be to become more like Jesus. Character will become more important than charisma; passion more important than personality.

The Lord is the Spirit; and where the Spirit of the Lord is, there is liberty. But we all, with unveiled face, beholding as in a mirror the glory of the Lord, are being transformed into the same image from glory to glory, just as by the Spirit of the Lord (2 Corinthians 3:17-18).

"Those who don't favor change will argue that teaching is enough, and will even say that worshiping churches are unbalanced because they are not emphasizing the teaching of God's Word. This, of course, is the opposite of what will be happening. Worshiping churches will be a place where worshipers will be thirsty for the Word and eager to hear it taught. The religious church will use the argument that Scripture is enough to change us without all the fuss about having to worship. This will appease some for a season, but then many will see the truth and run to seek His presence in worshiping churches.

Blessed is the man You choose, and cause to approach You, that he may dwell in Your courts. We shall be satisfied with the goodness of Your house, of Your holy temple (Psalm 65:4).

"Those who don't support such change will try and discourage and debase the real worship experience. They will say it borders on the cultish and demonic, but their actions will cause true worshipers to be even more diligent in seeking after God's presence, and more demonstrative in their unashamed worship of Him.

"The *convenience church* that characterized so much of the 1990s with a high degree of pre-planned service format and control, will soon start to give way to a spontaneous liberty of worship and the gifts of the Holy Spirit. This doesn't mean we won't plan our services, but it does mean there will be an openness and prayerful desire for the Holy Spirit to orchestrate the services the way He plans. Without doubt, this will be a challenging time for leaders as they let go of the reins and let the Spirit of God take charge. It will, however, bring them into a new place of trust and understanding of the work of the Holy Spirit, and it will reveal Jesus and the Father to them and their congregants in a greater way.

"Worship and those things that accompany it—such as salvation, healing, deliverance, warfare, and so on—will start to be understood and cause an excitement and expectancy among all who gather in His name. There will be almost no emphasis on formulating ways to attract the unbeliever because His presence will draw men and women from every walk of life and every ethnic background. Neither will there be any thought of appeasing unbelievers through special church programs designed not to offend them. In fact, the Word of God will be preached with such uncompromised boldness that it will be normal for the unbeliever to feel uncomfortable under the convicting power of the Holy Spirit, which will set them free. "You shall know the truth, and the truth shall make you free" (John 8:32).

"Entire congregations that are open to the move of God will be baptized in the Holy Spirit as they yield to Him."

Those who gladly received His Word were baptized; and that day about three thousand souls were added to them (Acts 2:41).

CHAPTER 10

A New Revelation of Power

When they began to sing and to praise, the Lord set ambushes against the people of Ammon, Moab, and Mount Seir, who had come against Judah; and they were defeated (2 Chronicles 20:22).

> "As praise and worship goes forth, the Word of the Lord shall be clearer to the listeners than it has ever been before. Pastors and teachers will be amazed at the growth and maturity of the worshipers, and God will receive all the glory for it."

In the story of King Jehoshaphat, something happened when God's people began to sing. The Lord went into action and brought defeat to their enemies. Also, in Acts, Paul and Silas started to sing and pray, and then suddenly God acted on their behalf and brought deliverance.

At midnight Paul and Silas were praying and singing hymns to God, and the prisoners were listening to them. Suddenly there was a great earthquake, so that the foundations of the prison were shaken; and immediately all the doors were opened and everyone's chains were loosed (Acts 16:25-26).

In both instances they were singing God's Word that had been sung years before. Jehoshaphat used the words that King David had sung at the dedication of the temple (see First Chronicles 16:34), and Paul was singing God's Word from Psalm 119:62.

"The Church is going to come into a new revelation of the power of God's Word when sung. We will see instant deliverances and manifestations of God's power when we praise. Worshipers will have such an insatiable capacity for God's Word, that it will lead to a growing demand for teachers. Churches will have to prepare for the influx not only of new converts but also of believers thirsty to hear more and more of God's Word. Those who are eager to hear the teaching of the Word will attend churches on a nightly basis. Leaders will request teachers from other denominations to come and help with the teaching, promoting the breakdown of many denominational barriers.

"During this time, God will raise up some of the most anointed teachers and preachers that the modern-day Church has ever seen. They will be an army of mighty warriors in the Kingdom, with the Word of God as their sharpened weapon, cutting asunder all the religious garbage of years gone by. They will bring such a prophetically clear message to the Church that the hearts and minds of the worshipers will be stirred to move by faith into greater exploits for God than they had ever dreamed possible. It will be common at that time for entire congregations to spontaneously rise from their seats during the preaching and teaching to give applause to God for the treasures contained in His Word. Leaders will be humbled by the revelation that is flowing from their mouths and the impact it is having on their people. This will cause congregations to worship for hours on end as a response to God's Word and the presence of His Spirit.

"The preaching of God's Word will be so anointed that often the preachers will be unable to finish the sermon because of spontaneous praise and worship. The reading of Scripture will be enough to spark spontaneous praise and hours of thanksgiving. Testimonies of the goodness of God will pour forth. Many meetings will be made up of saints testifying to the power of God in transformed lives and of deliverance from the forces of darkness. (See Psalm 107:1,8,15,21,31.) Amazed at the authenticity of such testimonies, leaders will fall on their knees in praise to God. In fact, many of the most powerful testimonies will come from leadership. At other times, congregations will sit in silent reverence and godly fear as God's Word is delivered or testimonies are given. A time of great wonder and amazement is about to sweep the Church as the Holy Spirit pours Himself out among all flesh.

"The unsaved will join the believers in worship, not really understanding what they are doing but knowing it is the right thing to do. Some will come under such conviction of God's love and compassion for them during the worship that they will commit their lives to Christ there and then. Many who have verbally and physically attacked the Church in the past will, like Saul, be converted without anyone even preaching to them.

"This atmosphere of God's presence will lead to amazing times of intercessory prayer in local churches as congregations cry out to God for the unsaved. Prayer meetings will run continuously as the Church gets a fresh revelation that we serve a God who answers prayer. Miraculous testimonies of answered prayer will stir people to pray even more, and prayer will become the basis of *God dreams* that come true.

> This atmosphere of God's presence will lead to amazing times of intercessory prayer in local churches as congregations cry out to God for the unsaved.

"God will add righteous, Word-saturated prayer warriors to churches to accomplish great assignments He has earmarked for local communities. Local communities will be shaken by the power of prayer unleashed through people who know their authority in Christ. Demonic strongholds in local communities that have caused pastors to quit will be routed through prayer and authoritative declarations and confessions. Many pastors and leaders will return to these areas and recover the spiritual and physical ground for Jesus that they had previously relinquished. Many communities will be covered like a blanket with God's Word through the confession, declaration, praise, and prayers of the saints. The power behind all of this will be the insatiable thirst for God's Word among believers.

"A heightened sense of compassion will bring about continuous prayer through groups committed and anointed to pray for the salvation of the family and friends of those in the church. Believers' unsaved friends and relatives will become known by name to the congregation as they cry out to God in prayer for their salvation. They will not cease in prayer and intercession until answers are received. The reality of an unsaved soul in eternal separation from God will send congregations to their knees in prayer for weeks and months until they see results. God will become known as the God who truly answers prayer, as opposed to the impotent gods of false religions. Prayer will become a strong foundation for every local church, and the trademark of churches worshiping their God in Spirit and in truth.

"In a short amount of time, more will be accomplished by these worshiping prayer warriors than by many previous generations. The things they achieve in the name of Jesus will bring fear to the hearts of men, causing them to turn toward God in repentance or run away from Him. At the same time, the demonic forces of darkness will prioritize their activities in the area of worship to the devil in a pathetic attempt to compete with God, but to no avail. Worship will be the priority in both the Kingdom of God and the kingdom of darkness but the prayers of the saints and their sacrificed lives will overcome the enemy.

"Prayer and praise based on God's Word will be the hallmark of the Church that will cause a quickening in events, propelling the Church forward in victory."

CHAPTER 11

Worshiping Children

The Lord came and stood and called as at other times, "Samuel! Samuel!" And Samuel answered, "Speak, for Your servant hears." Then the Lord said to Samuel: "Behold, I will do something in Israel at which both ears of everyone who hears it will tingle" (1 Samuel 3:10-11).

> "Get ready for a new wave of worship from children whose understanding of the things of God will overtake many who are unprepared. Godly children will separate themselves to praise and worship their Heavenly Father. They will follow those who not only teach worship but practice it as well."

In the midst of an evil world, God will make His children sensitive to hear His voice just as he did with Samuel when he was small. (See First Samuel 3:10-11;19-21.) Don't be surprised to hear profound messages coming from children including judgments that are coming on the earth. They will know God's voice and boldly declare what they have heard.

The Lord appeared again in Shiloh. For the Lord revealed Himself to Samuel in Shiloh by the word of the Lord (1 Samuel 3:21).

"As the Holy Spirit moves upon the children they will have intimate times with God in His presence that will astound their parents. They will have a revelation of God as a Father, impressed on them by the Holy Spirit. (See John 4:23-24.) Children touched by God in this way will start to separate themselves to worship and prayer at home and at school. At home, children will experience God intimately as they spend time in His Word, prayer, and praise. There will be no explanation for this except that it is a divine visitation from the Lord.

"Praise and worship will be a priority in children's church and will draw unsaved children because of the presence of God in their meetings. Children's ministry will have vibrant praise and worship as their central focus, and during this time young musicians will be raised up to lead praise for their own generation. The work of God in the lives of the children, especially through praise and worship, will be an example to adults and encourage them to press in to the things of God.

> The work of God in the lives of the children will be an example to adults and will encourage them to press in to the things of God.

"Children will have a tremendous desire to read God's Word. It will become apparent that where the truth of God's Word is taught, the Holy Spirit will cause the children to respond with praise and worship. Anointed children's church teachers will be raised up and recognized as vital to the church. These individuals will be highly sought after and characterized as worshipers who serve as living examples to the children. Many churches will be prepared to cope with the move of God among children. Those that are not will lose children and their parents to churches that are.

"Children's teachers who are not worshipers will experience increased discomfort in the midst of these worshiping children and will be motivated to become childlike in their relationship and response to God. Unwilling to adopt this childlike relationship with Jesus, some will resign, finding it unbearable to continue. The children will be moving as if in a river of God's presence. They will not wait for those who profess to be in the river but who are actually in a dry, desolate place. It will be a serious time to minister to children, and the Holy Spirit will not allow those who are engaging in an ungodly lifestyle or are insincere in their faith to continue in this ministry. Church leaders will be challenged to give the necessary priority to the children's ministry. God will not tolerate resistance or complacency in regard to this matter.

"Children will also have a compassion for the elderly, and this will be a significant area of evangelism. God's love will bridge the generation gap in a way that only He can. This will cause many elderly whose love for God has grown cold to recommit their lives to Him and become rejuvenated in new dimensions of service for the Kingdom. The elderly will be invited to attend youth meetings and many will respond and become *fathers and mothers in the faith* to the youth.

"Christian schools will experience a revival that will be way beyond our wildest imaginations. Praise and prayer meetings will take place continuously not only with the children but also the teachers and parents. Despite the efforts of some critics within the Church to stop this movement in the name of 'education,' the children will maintain their grades, and more importantly, experience changed hearts. Out of this will come a generation of leaders who will occupy positions in almost every field of endeavor, in both the church and the world. They will have godly wisdom that will be acknowledged throughout the entire earth.

"With secular schools also experiencing revival, even the critics of the movement will not be able to deny that something supernatural is taking place. Children will arrange praise and prayer meetings before school, during recess, and after school. Many children will be powerful witnesses for Christ, and great evangelistic crusades will be take place on the sports fields with children sharing testimonies to the goodness of God. Entire schools will be converted to Christ in a few days.

"During recess, inquisitive unsaved teachers will attend prayer and praise meetings held by the children and will be convicted and saved under the anointing that flows from the presence of the Holy Spirit. Many schools will experience the presence of the Holy Spirit at assembly times and to the amazement of everyone, children will be converted, healed, and delivered from all kinds of things. The name of Jesus will be the most known name in the school, which will lead to controversy over the issue of religious freedom in the public schools.

Christians will not have to fight for their rights to public prayer or worship as in the past, because it will be happening spontaneously as orchestrated by the Holy Spirit.

"Many secular schools will be virtually transformed into 'Christian' schools because of the work of the Holy Spirit. All the prayer that has been offered to God by faithful Christian parents and children will come to fruition in a quick and powerful way as the Holy Spirit sweeps through the public schools."

In Psalm 145:4, which says, "One generation shall praise Your works to another, and shall declare Your mighty acts," we are told to do our part in preparing for this great move among children. One generation—the adults—will praise God's miraculous works as a testimony to another generation—the children. It is God's intention that our children hear the great things He has done for us as adults. There is nothing more powerful to a child than the testimony of a parent, telling of God's faithfulness and goodness.

CHAPTER 12

A Worshiping Army of Children

Jesus said to them, "Yes. Have you never read, 'Out of the mouth of babes and nursing infants You have perfected praise?'" (Matthew 21:16)

"Children will go forth as a worshiping army that will astound even their teachers."

These remarkable young people will spend more and more time with their Bibles and Bible-illustrated books than their toys and games. Finally, Matthew 21:16 will be fulfilled. Jesus was quoting from Psalm 8:2, where the words *ordained strength* are used, but in Matthew, Jesus uses the words *perfected praise*. There is a praise coming from children that will release a powerful force in the spirit realm that will stop the enemy in his tracks.

Out of the mouth of babes and nursing infants You have ordained strength, because of Your enemies, that You may silence the enemy and the avenger (Psalm 8:2).

"Children will be used to silence the enemy, meaning that their praise will foil many of the devil's plans and purposes against the Church. Such will be the strength and power coming from the praises of the children.

"The move of God among the children will be so powerful across the face of the earth that it will be astounding to both parents and teachers alike. Children will be like a *specialized army of worshipers* that God has raised up for a strategic time. They will be well equipped to tear down the strongholds of the enemy with the simplicity of their prayers and praise."

Under the leadership of King Jehoshaphat, there was a time when the nation of Judah found itself surrounded by great armies that were about to destroy it. Jehoshaphat summoned the nation to seek God's help, and they stood before Him in family groups. "Now all Judah, with their little ones, their wives, and their children, stood before the Lord" (2 Chronicles 20:13).

The word *Judah* in the Hebrew means *to celebrate* or *to praise* God. The Scriptures state that all Judah stood before the Lord with their little ones and their children. The fathers are referred to as Judah, meaning praise. God defined the fathers as those who praised and celebrated Him. This is what a father is supposed to be—an example of praise to the rest of the family, especially the children.

Although it was the nation of Judah that came together, God refers to the nation as being made up of families. He refers to Judah (the fathers), the little ones (small children), wives (mothers), and children (teenagers). Because God is our Father, He is intensely interested in and deals with us at the family level. In the midst of these families standing before God seeking His deliverance, the Spirit comes and speaks through the prophet. "Thus says the Lord to you: Do not be afraid nor dismayed because of this great multitude, for the battle is not yours, but God's" (2 Chronicles 20:15).

> God is our Father, so He is intensely interested in and deals with us at the family level.

These are the same words the Spirit is speaking to us as families—"do not be afraid." This is surely a prophetic message for us in these end times. We should stand with our families and seek God's face for deliverance from all the enemies that come against us. The parents must have reinforced the words of the prophet before the battle took place to assure their children of God's protection and deliverance. After the Lord defeated the enemy on Judah's behalf, the children would have recounted the story of God's promises and His faithfulness.

This is a prophetic picture of our children who will have no fear of the enemy because they will know the promises of God and His faithfulness to keep them.

Chapter 13

Revival Among Children

Little children were brought to Him that He might put His hands on them and pray, but the disciples rebuked them. But Jesus said, "Let the little children come to Me, and do not forbid them; for of such is the kingdom of heaven." And He laid His hands on them and departed from there (Matthew 19:13-15).

> "Don't ever discourage their worship or stop the flow. Encourage the children as they stand before God and worship Him."

"God is about to release a revival spirit among our children. To be effective as pastors, leaders, children's ministers, and parents in such a time, we will need to develop a keen sensitivity to what God is requiring of us in order for Him to do this work among the children. Leaders who fail to seriously consider this work of God will encounter significant difficulties and face the prospect of fading to a place of insignificance in the Kingdom.

"In churches where leadership resists God's leading, efforts to bear fruit in other areas of ministry will be frustrated, regardless of the time and energy invested in them. It will become a fearful thing to prioritize a personal agenda ahead of God's.

"In contrast to this, leaders who sense God's hand upon the children will prioritize their ministry on equal footing with everything else in the life of the church. As they encourage the children to worship the Lord, they will start to experience the favor of God in every other area."

Jesus warned the disciples that they should not forbid the children to come to Him.

> *They brought little children to Him, that He might touch them; but the disciples rebuked those who brought them. But when Jesus saw it, He was greatly displeased and said to them, "Let the little children come to Me, and do not forbid them; for of such is the kingdom of God. Assuredly, I say to you, whoever does not receive the kingdom of God as a little child will by no means enter it." And He took them up in His arms, laid His hands on them, and blessed them* (Mark 10:13-16).

We see from this Scripture that Jesus showed open displeasure when His disciples tried to stop parents from bringing their children to Him. His rebuke to them is a warning to us. He loves little children, and we must make room to bring them to Him. His message is twofold:

1. We must be childlike in order to receive God's Kingdom.

2. He will establish His Kingdom through the children.

Parents bring their children to church, but the church must ensure that the children are given every opportunity to receive the blessings Jesus has for them.

"At times children will lead worship in the adult services and usher in the presence of God with accompanying preaching and powerful testimonies that will greatly touch congregations. The presence and flow of the Holy Spirit in these meetings will be so tangible that there will be no doubt God has His hand on the children and has chosen to use them in a most profound way. All this will truly astound their teachers and parents as God revives His children."

CHAPTER 14

Skillful and Anointed Musicians

All these were under the direction of their father for the music in the house of the Lord, with cymbals, stringed instruments, and harps, for the service of the house of God. Asaph, Jeduthun, and Heman were under the authority of the king....And they cast lots for their duty, the small as well as the great, the teacher with the student (I Chronicles 25:6,8).

> "Musicians will stand in line, totally submitted to pastors and music directors waiting for the opportunity to serve in the house of the Lord. Chief musicians will train them, and God will give those involved in music ministry the capacity to receive the equipping and anointing He intends for them."

"The Lord is presently raising up a new generation of music ministers who will be humble and submissive to local church leadership. They will also be among some of the most anointed in the history of the Church. Just as was King David, they will be led by the Holy Spirit."

Samuel took the horn of oil and anointed him in the midst of his brothers; and the Spirit of the Lord came upon David from that day forward. So Samuel arose and went to Ramah (1 Samuel 16:13).

"These music ministers will be known for high standards of righteousness, integrity, humility, and faithfulness, which will reflect the depth and intensity of their personal time with God. Their ministry will simply be an extension of who they are as worshipers. Intimacy with God will be their foremost characteristic. Church leadership will allow them opportunity to continue to seek the Lord as part of their *normal* daily duties.

"Finances will be released into local churches for music ministers to be employed full-time, allowing them to meditate on God's Word, pray, and worship as part of their accepted role in the life of the church."

These are the singers, heads of the fathers' houses of the Levites, who lodged in the chambers, and were free from other duties; for they were employed in that work day and night (1 Chronicles 9:33).

"The music ministers' prayer lives will be strong, and they will quickly become recognized as one of the most effective ministries in the church. As a result of their lifestyle of prayer and worship, they will hear melodies sung in Heaven and introduce these to the church on earth. As the whole Church begins to tune in to heavenly worship, a unity with the heavenly worshipers will be experienced. This will be the precursor to a release of heavenly power such as the world has not experienced since the time of Jesus. We will sing of His power and strength as it literally impacts the earth. As Psalm 21:13 says: "Be exalted, O Lord, in Your own strength! We will sing and praise Your power.""

"These singers and musicians will also be fearless warriors with the high praise of God in their mouths and two-edged swords in their hands, leading congregations into powerful seasons of warfare with decisive results against the enemy."

> As we tune into heavenly worship, it will cause a release of heavenly power on the earth.

Let the high praises of God be in their mouth, and a two-edged sword in their hand, to execute vengeance on the nations, and punishments on the peoples; to bind their kings with chains, and their nobles with fetters of iron; to execute on them the written judgment—this honor have all His saints. Praise the Lord! (Psalm 149:6-9)

"Blockages that have hindered the Church for years will be removed quickly when the Church unites in anointed warfare. Pastors and leaders will often join with the musicians and singers and lead their congregations into battle.

"Some in the music ministry will be anointed with a strong prophetic mantle that God will use to provide clear direction to the local church. As a result of this, there will be little need for local churches to copy the programs of other successful ministries. Leaders will be hearing God's guidance through the prophetic mantle operating in their own churches.

"Music ministers will have a supernatural ability to receive and implement what the Lord is doing in their lives because of the tender condition of their hearts for God. Like King David, they will have a heart after God and the anointing of the Holy Spirit will operate strongly through them. (See First Samuel 16:13.) They will have an acute understanding of the flow of the Holy Spirit in services, and along with leadership, will usher congregations into the awesome presence of God. The church will literally be bathed day and night with God's presence.

"Churches saturated in this atmosphere of praise and worship and the undeniable presence of God will draw congregations. It will become commonplace for the sick to be instantly healed as they enter such churches.

"The preaching of God's Word, and anointed worship interspersed with silence and a contentment to just sit and bask in the presence of God, will become common.

"Initially there will be a short supply of anointed musicians, causing church leaders to seek them out. God will address this by raising up worship training centers around the world to train both musicians and singers. These training centers will focus not only on music and worship but also on prayer and meditation on God's Word. Graduates of these unique schools will be highly sought after because they will not only be skillfull in music but also in the things of the Spirit and the Word."

Chapter 15

Creative Ministers Separated to God

David and the captains of the army separated for the service
some of the sons of Asaph, of Heman, and of Jeduthun, who
should prophesy with harps, stringed instruments, and cymbals
(1 Chronicles 25:1).

> "These musicians will stand apart from sinful worldly
> music and their lives will speak clearly of separation
> unto God."

In this chapter, though specific reference is often made to music
ministry, the prophecy should be considered to apply indirectly to all
creative ministries. All are being afforded greater recognition and priority in the Church, and this trend must continue.

One of the tragedies of music ministers is that so many of them
have been abused, misused, misunderstood, and to a certain extent, ig-
nored by church leadership. The root of the problem for some lies in
the fact that they were chosen because of their talent and not their
anointing, their ability rather than their intimacy with God. They have
subsequently been hurt and have tired of the church's hypocrisy and
politics. This has caused much heartache to both the musician and the
leadership, mostly because insufficient time was given to mentoring
and developing relationships. This is, however, changing, and church

leaders are developing stronger relationships with these ministers, bringing them into a unity of purpose in glorifying God.

"Memories of the shortcomings of individuals in this ministry will fade as a new breed of musicians and singers comes forth, living their lives in accordance with the standards God has prescribed in His Word. They will exhibit righteousness and holiness along with excellence in musical skills. Obviously great musicians won't be present in every church, but where a genuine hunger for God through worship is sought and practiced, anointed music ministers will be found. God's standard for music ministry is high, with no room for compromise. There will be an increased acceptance of mentoring and training in the things of the Word and the Spirit as essential precursors to releasing these gifted people into effective, fruitful ministry."

In King David's time, the musicians and singers were appointed and also separated to do their ministry.

David spoke to the leaders of the Levites to appoint their brethren to be the singers accompanied by instruments of music, stringed instruments, harps, and cymbals, by raising the voice with resounding joy (1 Chronicles 15:16).

The Hebrew meaning of these words shows they were chosen to minister to God and separated specifically for that purpose. They wore white linen ephods, the same type the High Priest wore under his garments. It represented their separated service and life of righteousness. Righteous living will release a fresh and new anointing through creative ministers. God has always used creative people to build His tabernacles and the Temple. (See First Chronicles 22:15-16.) They are part of His building plan and have an anointing to prepare a place for His presence inside and outside the church.

"Creative ministers are emerging with a new confidence and boldness because of the recognition by leadership of God's calling on their lives and talents and this ministry's place in the Church. God's presence will also be communicated through creative ministries and will be recognized even by the world. It will be evident in all their creative skills, such as art, music, dancing, and photography, for example, that what they are producing creatively is supernatural. God's presence will be released through them and their creative output."

Creative ministries are absolutely part of God's plan not only to minister to Him but also to attract the unsaved to Him.

"Many will be drawn to the church through these evangelistically anointed and creatively gifted ministries."

One of the significant features of these ministers is their ability to communicate with God through their worship and with man through their gifts. The church needs these ministries to expose the creativity of God, not only in the church but also to the world. This will draw many people to receive Jesus and, in a sense, they'll be preparing a place for Him to reside in the hearts of men. They will be drawn to churches that appreciate their calling, mentor them in righteousness, and encourage them with their gift.

"Many talented people in the world live shameful lifestyles. Their behavior has been accepted as normal because of their artistic skills, but those in the church will exhibit the opposite lifestyles of godliness and holiness. They will stand apart from sinful worldly music, and their lives will speak clearly of separation unto God.

"Musicians and singers, along with other creative ministers, will be affiliated with others throughout the world, exchanging new songs and ideas regularly. The most important meetings they arrange, however, will be events where their sole purpose is to worship the living God. These worship events will draw leaders and laymen alike and bring down the kingdoms of darkness in cities across the earth. Leaders will target certain cities for these worship events to take place. These will cause tremendous breakthroughs in the Body of Christ. Although these worship meetings are not designed as soul-winning events, many will be drawn to them and find Christ as Lord. In fact creative ministries will be at the forefront of a new wave of evangelism never previously seen or imagined. Musicians will move in a strong prophetic and healing ministry that will make the devil tremble at the sound of their praise and declarations of God's Word.

"The secular world of music will start to pay attention to these Christian musicians because of the wonderful melodies and power that is associated with them, and will attempt to buy them off. Some will fall prey to this but most of them will grow stronger in their conviction to serve the Lord and Him only. Their lives will become increasingly sold-out and separated unto God and their righteous living will stand in stark contrast to the ungodly lifestyle of many secular musicians. Music will become more than just 'music' as we know it today, reflecting the lifestyles of those who perform it both in the secular world and the Church. An increasing decadence will exemplify the music and musicians in the world as opposed to the righteous living that will be evident in the lives of God's musicians and worshipers."

Leaders are realizing that creative ministry is one of the most important ministries within the Church, and it is being given its proper recognition and rightful place. There is a great future ahead for creative people who are nurtured under true fathers in the faith. The seeds sown in their lives will bring forth a harvest way beyond anything imaginable as God releases His anointing through them.

CHAPTER 16

A Great Time for Missions

[God] has put a new song in my mouth—praise to our God;
many will see it and fear, and will trust in the Lord (Psalm 40:3).

"Schools will be established specifically to set a standard for worship in the congregations. Psalmody schools will start all over the world to train the Body of Christ, psalmists, and worship leaders. These schools will flourish like flowers in the desert after the rain, where no man has planted and no man has watered but only God has prospered. The students from these schools will soon become the teachers and the original teachers will move on."

Since this prophecy was spoken, this has begun to be fulfilled. Course material from the Psalmody School of Worship has been implemented in more than 30 nations.

"There will be a continual movement throughout the world of holy men and women with an overwhelming desire and objective to exemplify praise and worship. In these glorious times, God will stir up a desire in the hearts of men and women to get up and go as missionaries to the ends of the world. As they worship, they will be overcome and propelled by the love of God for the lost. Missionaries will be raised up among the most unexpected people. Young people just graduating from school will go to the mission field. Many who have settled into retirement will travel to nations to preach the Gospel and help with the work of the Lord. Successful business executives will make time to go. Families will use their vacation time for missionary trips, and youth and children's groups will go during school holidays.

"Christian businesspeople will be actively involved in missionary projects through local churches, providing finances and support for those who go to the nations to preach the Gospel. Local churches will be inundated by those who volunteer to go and by the generosity of those who can't.

> Local churches will be inundated by those who volunteer to go to the mission field and by the generosity of those who can't.

"It will be a wonderful time for missions, and the greatest harvest ever reaped will be seen in these times through both laymen and leaders. The outstanding significance of these missionaries will be their love for God and their understanding of His presence as they have discovered Him in prayer and worship.

"Due to the sophisticated communication available through the Internet, most missionaries will have instant prayer support for anything they request from the local church. There will be dedicated prayer warriors whose sole function will be to continuously cover missionaries in prayer. A highly organized global network of intercessors and prayer warriors will make use of the advanced communication systems God has given to ensure that any missionary who wants prayer will receive it day and night.

"An outstanding characteristic of prayer will be the dimension of victorious praise that accompanies it, causing things to change quite suddenly in the spirit realm and subsequently in the natural realm. Prayer and praise will be so united as one dynamic force that we will reflect with amazement on the results that this synergy brings."

God allows us to pray so we can fellowship with Him. The part *God* loves is the fellowship that prayer enables us to have with Him. The part *we* love is the answers that prayer brings. This is why Jesus taught His disciples to open their prayer with "our Father." This is addressing God in the most intimate way. A revelation of God as our loving Father is the key to addressing God in prayer.

As the Church matures, it will understand and enjoy the fellowship part of prayer more and more. There is great reward for those who have learned not to simply rush into prayer with their requests, but take time to approach God worshipfully before making requests, always closing with thanksgiving. Many powerful saints of God know this se-cret, and get their prayers answered. One great man of God said, "I used to pray long and praise little in my time with God, but now my prayers are shorter and my praise is longer." The man found the secret of enhancing his prayer with thanksgiving and praise. Jesus will return for a worshiping Church that knows how to pray.

CHAPTER 17
Abundance to Build the Kingdom

O Lord our God, all this abundance that we have prepared to build You a house for Your holy name is from Your hand, and is all Your own (1 Chronicles 29:16).

> "The Most High God will identify their job description as worshipers, and they will have no need of anything the world can offer."

"One of the features of the Church will be that believers will be absolutely sold out to God and completely dedicated to His Kingdom. Faith for finances will abound in the lives of the saints and many businesspeople will be raised up as multi-millionaires in a relatively short time. Others who are trusting God for a release of finances to bless the Kingdom will receive inheritances from sources they did not expect."

God promises that those who love Him will inherit wealth. He tells us it is available to those who seek Him. It is found where the paths of righteousness and justice intersect.

I love those who love me, and those who seek me diligently will find me. Riches and honor are with me, enduring riches and righteousness. My fruit is better than gold, yes, than fine gold, and my revenue than choice silver. I traverse the way of righteousness, in the midst of the paths of justice, that I may cause those who love me to inherit wealth, that I may fill their treasuries (Proverbs 8:17-21).

> One of the features of the Church will be her absolute sellout to God and total dedication to the Kingdom.

"Supernatural abundance will follow worshipers who have a heart to use finances and resources to establish the Kingdom throughout the earth. They will have no need of anything that the world can offer and will in no way sell out or be bought by the world's wealth or glitter. Jesus will be their portion, and they will only seek Him for all of their needs.

"God will supply according to His riches in glory, and wealth will abound in local churches to supply the financial needs of the work of the Lord. Where there is a heart and mind to establish God's Kingdom based on His covenant, the power to get wealth will operate through those He can trust.

> *You shall remember the Lord your God, for it is He who gives you power to get wealth, that He may establish His covenant which He swore to your fathers, as it is this day* (Deuteronomy 8:18).

"Large financial institutions and corporations will be owned by godly people and will push the Church forward. The spirit of lack will be only a memory in the Church as God gives the power to get wealth to establish His Kingdom. Combined with a willingness of heart to serve the Lord with gladness, there will be an abundance of wealth and people resources to undertake what the Church has been called to do. Like the wise men who visited Jesus at His birth, we will come to worship Him and lay down our treasures at His feet. All this will be a result of His presence in our midst.

"The Church will take on a mantle of prosperity that will get the world's attention. To the envy of many, the largest indoor buildings in the world will belong to local churches, but this will bring positive attention to the church. Spiritual abundance builds the Church but so does natural abundance."

> *O Lord our God, all this abundance that we have prepared to build You a house for Your holy name is from Your hand, and is all Your own* (1 Chronicles 29:16).

"The spirit of lack that has plagued the Church with a poverty mentality will fight against the worshiping Church and will be one of the strongholds we will have to face, but it will be conquered. It will succumb and be replaced by the generous Holy Spirit whom God has poured out abundantly through Jesus Christ our Savior."

CHAPTER 18
Known by Love

By this all will know that you are My disciples, if you have love for one another (John 13:35).

"They will be known by their love and loved by their knowing."

"Worship will be the most outstanding hallmark of the Church and will identify those who are in Christ as opposed to those who profess to be but are not. Even the unconverted will see the love that Christians have for Jesus and the love and sacrifice they offer those who don't know Him. The Church will be identified more than anything by her love and her faith. Love will be our calling card to the world and faith will be our gift to them.

"The world will at first mock many charitable deeds done in the name of Christ, but will soon realize that they are genuine, selfless acts of love that have never been displayed by any other religious group. They will also realize that Christians cannot be intimidated or defeated in their mission to preach the Gospel to the world. They will see that they are dealing with a generation of *lovers of God* that the world has not encountered before on such a massive global scale. God's love will prevail both in and out of the Church, and the Scripture, 'love never fails,' will become a reality for the Church. (See First Corinthians 13:8.)"

> National leaders will openly ask worshiping prayer warriors to call on God to avert wars and impending natural disasters.

To accomplish great Kingdom exploits for God, we need great faith. The devil tries to stop our faith, and he does it by stopping our love. Our first love for God is demonstrated in worship. This is where faith is incubated and then birthed by loving one another. If our faith is not functioning, we must look at where we stand in our love for others, and more specifically our love for God as expressed through worship. There is little hope for our world unless the Church exercises its first love by worshiping Jesus. The unchurched will not be attracted by our works or our endurance but by our love. (See Revelation 2:1-7.) Worshiping God is such a key to winning the community because love is released in the neighborhood environment, opening up the opportunity for great faith in healing, miracles, and wonders.

To God, worship is not an end in itself, but a means to an end. The purpose of worship is misunderstood by many and therefore not as highly prioritized as it should be. God is not seeking worship—He is seeking those who engage in worship. God primarily created man to worship Him, and it must be the most fulfilling spiritual exercise of all. Worship achieves two things:

1) We fulfill the purpose of our existence when we do it.

2) We fulfill God's purpose for the Kingdom.

God has a purpose for His Kingdom. It is that His will be done in earth as it is in Heaven by the presence and power of the Holy Spirit working through Christians.

Since we are receiving a kingdom which cannot be shaken, let us have grace, by which we may serve God acceptably with reverence and godly fear. For our God is a consuming fire (Hebrews 12:28-29).

The Kingdom of God cannot be shaken, moved, or altered in any way. Everything has to submit to its infinite power. We have the amazing privilege as Kingdom citizens to rule the Kingdom here on earth with all of Heaven's power to back us. The Scripture above gives us insight into how we should respond. We need grace to grasp the privilege of what we have been given and then respond with worship. The Greek word for *serve* in this context also means *to worship*. Our first step in serving God as Kingdom citizens is to worship Him in reverence and godly fear. We are reminded that God is a consuming fire—alluding to the fact that He will not tolerate Kingdom activity from those who don't revere Him with godly fear.

Love guarantees that the Church will have a glorious future.

CHAPTER 19

Supernatural Strength to Minister

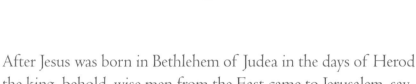

After Jesus was born in Bethlehem of Judea in the days of Herod the king, behold, wise men from the East came to Jerusalem, saying, "Where is He who has been born King of the Jews? For we have seen His star in the East and have come to worship Him" (Matthew 2:1-2).

> "These men and women will have a supernatural ability to work and travel, to uproot, adapt, and resettle, to move quickly and be highly efficient."

Over the centuries, God has consistently sent His people out to far and distant lands for the sake of the Kingdom. Some of the most esteemed servants of God have done their greatest work in foreign nations. God has given them a supernatural love, strength, and adaptability to uproot, travel, and resettle.

"Mission activity will increase, and because of faster modes of travel, believers will be moving around the earth constantly and with relative ease. Missionary teams will fly halfway around the world for short ministry trips. They will be fresh to minister when they arrive, returning a few days later with a supernatural strength from on high because of the prayer support of the saints. They will have a supernatural empowerment from the Lord enabling them to work extremely hard and to achieve much during these times. Likewise, in many local churches leaders will be able to preach multiple services in a way they could not have before, as the Holy Spirit strengthens them. A supernatural strength will empower God's people as they worship. (See Psalm 59:17.)

"God will move His people around the world to establish His work and many will be called who never expected to be used in ministry. New converts will support many ministers who travel, and God will use their testimonies to reach the lost.

"Religious people think they have found God, ignorant people don't know there is a God to find, but wise people know there is a time to seek Jesus and prepare for the journey that will take them into His presence. This is happening right now in the churches where wise men and women assemble."

At the time of Jesus' birth, wise men left their comfortable homes and familiar surroundings and travelled a long distance to worship Jesus. They were motivated by the fact that the Scriptures had prophesied His birth. They sacrificed much for the privilege and opportunity to worship Him. These were leaders, men of intellect and the greatest scholars of their day, but they humbled themselves, laid aside their own natural wisdom, and followed a star. They were determined that whatever the cost, they would find Him and worship Him. They were prophetic in the sense that they knew the season of His birth, and they had prepared for that moment. "When they had come into the house, they saw the child with Mary His mother, and fell down and worshiped Him" (Matthew 2:11).

Just as the wise men of old humbly laid aside their position and intellect, wise leaders in today's Church are likewise leaving the comfortable and familiar to seek Jesus and worship Him no matter the cost. Personal agendas are being exchanged for God's agendas, and man-made ideas are being abandoned for God ideas. We are entering a time when all of us will be challenged to travel into spiritual territory, which may be unfamiliar. But it is within such territory that we will find His presence. Wise men and women still seek Him, no matter what it takes to find Him.

CHAPTER 20
God Is Glorified

I have glorified You on the earth. I have finished the work which You have given Me to do (John 17:4).

"They will bring glory and honor to the Most High God wherever they go and will never be glorified themselves. The servant's attitude of these men and women will touch even the ungodly, and they will become known as worshiping servants who are loved and highly respected."

"Humility will be the normal order in the Church and leaders will be found in a continuous place of seeking God for further purification of heart."

> ...Do you think that the Scripture says in vain, "The Spirit who dwells in us yearns jealously"? But He gives more grace. Therefore He says: "God resists the proud, but gives grace to the humble." Therefore submit to God. Resist the devil and he will flee from you. Draw near to God and He will draw near to you. Cleanse your hands, you sinners; and purify your hearts, you double-minded (James 4:5-8).

Grace is God's ability to do supernatural accomplishments through a heart that is constantly purified by God's Word. Grace multiplies as we gain more knowledge of God's Word, meaning that God's ability accelerates as we meditate and spend time in His presence. The outpouring of grace will allow local church pastors and leaders to achieve seemingly impossible things in local congregations and communities.

Grace and peace be multiplied to you in the knowledge of God and of Jesus our Lord (2 Peter 1:2).

"The humility of these men and women will be obvious to everyone, and they will preach that it is only by the grace of God that they are partakers of His plan and purpose for the Church. All those who serve God in this hour will have a tremendous sense of the privilege they have been given to be born at such a strategic time in Church history and indeed the history of the world. This will stem from the reality confirmed in our hearts that we are living close to the end of this dispensation of the Church age, and that God has favored us to bring the message of the Gospel at the end.

"The grace of God operating in the lives of believers at this time will cause them to reach out with compassion to others inside and outside the Church. It will be a season of God graciously pouring out His love to the world through His chosen channel, the Church.

"Pride that has ravaged the Church and stripped her of some of her chosen servants will no longer be found therein. It will be replaced by humility. The servant heart of believers will reveal Jesus to the world in a way they have not seen Him before, and it will bring Him glory and honor. As the Church serves the world with loving-kindness, many will respond because they have seen Jesus through these loved and highly respected men and women."

Every person craves love, peace, hope, and prosperity, and the Church carries these to the world. These values distinguish us from the world, and are what humanity at large is seeking.

Jesus said He glorified the Father by finishing the work He had given Him to do. (See John 17:4.)

It is important to understand what it means to glorify God. Not only is it working for Him but also sitting at His feet watching and listening to Him. Martha worked hard, thinking that Jesus was hungry for food. She failed to realize that she was the hungry one. Her sister Mary's work was to sit and devour Jesus' Words.

It happened as they went that He entered a certain village; and a certain woman named Martha welcomed Him into her house. And she had a sister called Mary, who also sat at Jesus' feet and heard His word. But Martha was distracted with much serving, and she approached Him and said, "Lord, do You not care that my sister has left me to serve alone? Therefore tell her to help me." And Jesus answered and said to her, "Martha, Martha, you are worried and troubled about many things. But one thing is needed, and Mary has chosen that good part, which will not be taken away from her" (Luke 10:38-42).

The mistake so many in the Church have made is to work for Jesus in the kitchen when He was calling them to the living room. The world is suffering as a result. The greatest work that lies ahead for the Church is not in the streets but in the prayer and worship closet. That is where we'll find Jesus serving us with the spiritual food we need to feed the world.

Jesus said that Mary chose the good part, sitting at His feet hearing the message of the Kingdom. Glorifying God starts with hearing the Word, then doing it. The work of the Kingdom has to be the consequence of the message. Then the emphasis will be righteousness and the Kingdom, just as Jesus preached when He began His ministry. "Seek first the kingdom of God and His righteousness, and all these things shall be added to you" (Matthew 6:33).

Righteousness is right standing with God. It is positioning us to operate as kings and priests who have the authority to rule on this earth because we operate as priests who serve God in prayer and worship and obedience to His Word. Everything the Church needs will be supplied to a righteous people.

The five-fold ministry of apostles, prophets, evangelists, pastors, and teachers glorify God when they sit at the feet of Jesus. This is the work leaders are being called to. It is out of this place of intimacy with Him that they will effectively feed the sheep and empower them to do Kingdom work.

Kingdom work will be most effective when God's nature and character are openly evident in the lives of His people. He will then truly be glorified because the world will see Jesus in us.

CHAPTER 21

In Awe of God

All the ends of the world shall remember and turn to the Lord, and all the families of the nations shall worship before You. For the kingdom is the Lord's and He rules over the nations (Psalm 22:27-28).

> "All this will be such a work of the Holy Spirit that no one will take any credit. Even the five-fold ministry (apostles, prophets, evangelist, pastors, and teachers) will melt into the congregation as we all stand before God in adoration and awe."

"In this move of God, it will be so obvious to everyone that credit cannot be ascribed to any particular person, church, or denomination. It will be regarded as a sovereign move of God in the Church. It will be characterized by openness to the Holy Spirit and His work through believers. The presence and power of God will be far greater than anything we could compare it with in previous times and will overshadow all the revivals in Church history since the Book of Acts.

"It's never easy to make adjustments to accommodate the move of His Spirit but it has to be done. Leaders and churches that refuse to seek and prioritize God's presence through worship, prayer, and faith in God's Word will experience serious times of chastisement from the Lord.

"There will be no place for leaders who are not passionate about God and thirsty for Him. Ministries and ministers with selfish motives will be exposed by the Holy Spirit through their lack of humility, disingenuous worship, and limited intimacy with God. Soon they will be unable to serve. Eventually many leaders will turn to the Lord in repentance, and God in His grace will restore them to a greater ministry than before. Some, however, will be left out in the cold, still resistant to the flow of the Spirit. Sadly, their own actions will disqualify them to partake in the greatest move of God of all time.

> *The presence and power of God will be far greater than anything we have known in previous times and will overshadow all the revivals in church history since the Book of Acts.*

"The thirst for God and righteous living among leaders will impact their homes in particular as marriages and relationships are restored. This will spill over into the Church and bring about a healing of relationships among leaders in the same towns and cities. Many of these things are already happening, but it is only a trickle compared to the flood that will come.

"Leaders will love God more than they love preaching sermons about Him. Their passion for God will draw people into their churches to seek a relationship with God. True leadership in the Church will be demonstrated not so much as the ability to preach or organize, but as the capacity to love God.

"Passion will be the hallmark of the end-time Church, based upon a revelation of His love for us. This will cause an unquenchable thirst for more of Him. A revelation of God's love is about to sweep us into previously unknown realms of worship within the Church and evangelistic transformations outside of it."

It is my hope that this prophetic word encourages all of us to consider the true motives and purpose of what we are doing in church. This applies especially to leaders who will face a more severe judgment by

God. "My brethren, let not many of you become teachers, knowing that we shall receive a stricter judgment. For we all stumble in many things. If anyone does not stumble in word, he is a perfect man, able also to bridle the whole body" (James 3:1-2).

Please take this word as an encouragement that God has singled you out for this moment in the history of the Church. You are unique and of infinite value to God as He builds His Kingdom. This psalm sums up all that I have attempted to convey in this book. May it be a blessing to you.

All the ends of the world shall remember and turn to the Lord, and all the families of the nations shall worship before You. For the kingdom is the Lord's and He rules over the nations (Psalm 22:27-28).

PART TWO

PRACTICAL INSIGHTS INTO WORSHIP

CHAPTER 1
Created to Worship

When you worship you are fulfilling the purpose for your existence. Everything else is peripheral to this and should be a consequence of it.

God does nothing without purpose, and you are God's purpose on the earth today. Scripture says that you are His treasured possession, or, it could be said, His treasured purpose.

You are a people holy to the Lord your God. The Lord your God has chosen you out of all the peoples on the face of the earth to be his people, his treasured possession (Deuteronomy 7:6 NIV).

The plan He has for your life is infinitely valuable to Him and those you will come in contact with. You could have existed a hundred or a thousand years ago, but God in His wisdom decided to create you for His purposes at this time in human history. God said you are created to worship. He couldn't think of a better reason for your existence, so there must be something extremely life-fulfilling in the act of worship. Isaiah 43:21 says: "This people have I formed for Myself; they shall show forth My praise."

At that time God was referring to the nation of Israel, but now He is referring to you. "You are a chosen generation, a royal priesthood, a holy nation, His own special people, that you may proclaim the praises of Him who called you out of darkness into His marvellous light" (1 Peter 2:9).

There's nothing God treasures more than you and nothing He desires more from you than worship. When you worship you are fulfilling the purpose of your existence. Everything else is peripheral to this and should be a consequence of your worship of God. A worshiper is priceless in the eyes of God.

YOU ARE ON GOD'S MIND

The Father chose us even before He created the universe. As Ephesians 1:4 says: "He chose us in Him before the foundation of the world, that we should be holy and without blame before Him in love."

He knew us before we were actually born. (See Jeremiah 1:4-5.) There has never been a time in eternity past or present when you were not in God's thoughts. Because of the love He has for you, your life occupies His mind at all times. He's thinking about you now, even as you read this book. John 4:23 says that the Father is seeking worshipers. It gives us the impression that this is a continual search concerning your life right now.

The hour is coming, and now is, when the true worshipers will worship the Father in spirit and truth; for the Father is seeking such to worship Him (John 4:23).

The most humbling thing to realize is that God Almighty who runs the universe loves you so much that He is continually knocking at the door of your heart seeking your worship. He does it not because He needs it, but because you need to give it. It's your purpose for living, and He knows that life makes no sense without it. Life without worship is like a fish without water. The source of its existence has been removed, and it eventually suffocates. Worship is the environment of God's presence, and we struggle in life without it.

Some may think that being in the clergy is important to God and it is, but it's not the most important thing. If it were, we would all be created to become vocational ministers—which we aren't. We are, however, all created to worship and from that flows ministry in its many forms.

You were created to worship, not just once or twice a week at church, but as a lifestyle. If worship is not a lifestyle for you, it stands to reason that you might feel like something is missing at church. God expects us to worship Him at all times. What is in your mouth proceeds from what is in your heart, or more accurately, your mind. Consider Psalm 34:1: "I will bless the Lord at all times; His praise shall continually be in my mouth."

Worship is simply a gauge to measure what we think of God. A lifestyle of praise flows from a mind that is continually renewed and filled with hope in God's promises. "I will hope continually, and will praise You yet more and more. My mouth shall tell of Your righteousness and Your salvation all the day, for I do not know their limits" (Psalm 71:14-15).

We see here that the psalmist caught a glimpse of God's limitless saving grace toward him and his only response was to praise Him more and more. We are all created to discover His righteousness and appreciate His saving grace so that we can worship Him more and more.

WORSHIP AFFECTS YOUR DESTINY

God has a great plan and purpose for your life, and that plan and purpose is fulfilled as a consequence of worship. "I know the thoughts that I think toward you, says the Lord, thoughts of peace and not of evil, to give you a future and a hope" (Jeremiah 29:11).

The fullness of our destiny is graciously withheld from us until we learn to worship. Attempting to carry out God's plan without worship is possibly the greatest contributing factor for failure in life. Indeed, it is probably one of the main contributing factors in the lives of those who fall from ministry due to a misalignment of priorities. Working for God is what you are called to do, not what you are created to do. We will never know how many failures and unfulfilled dreams can be traced back to a lack of worship, but we do know that when we worship Him, we are set to discover the plans and purposes He has for us, and how to fulfill them.

Blessed is the man who walks not in the counsel of the ungodly, nor stands in the path of sinners, nor sits in the seat of the scornful; but his delight is in the law of the Lord, and in His law he meditates day and night (Psalm 1:1-2).

The psalmist delighted (strongly desired and longed) for God's Word. It gave him a sense of pleasure, purpose, and direction. We cannot delight in something without having a sense of praise for it. Delighting in something or someone is the forerunner to praise. It is because he meditated on God's Word that the psalmist took the right paths in life.

Walking the right way in life is not a choice of paths; it's a choice of books. When you meditate on God's Word, He'll meditate on you. When you delight in Him, He'll delight in you. The time you spend with God is directly related to the time He will spend with you. When you delight in God's Word, you will always get to the right place at the right time and do the right things with the right people. Nothing secures your destiny in God more than delighting in God's Word with thanksgiving, praise, and worship on your lips.

> Attempting to carry out God's plans without worship is possibly the greatest contributing factor for failure in life.

YOUR WORSHIP IS UNIQUE

Believe it or not, the world has never experienced anyone quite like you. Even more astonishing is the fact that neither has God. Scripture confirms this in Isaiah 43:7, "Everyone who is called by My name, whom I have created for My glory; I have formed him, yes, I have made him."

The Hebrew word for created is *bara* and emphasizes *producing something new and perfect out of the ordinary*, such as a masterpiece. The fact is that God has never made another you. Every individual who has ever lived or lives today is unique. God's love for each individual is so great that He has never made any two individuals the same throughout the history of the human race. There is nothing new to God, with one exception—you. He's never previously experienced a "worshiping you" and He never will again.

Though many of us spend our lives comparing ourselves with others, God never does. You respond to Him like no one else does. Your relationship with Him is unique. He has millions of worshipers but only one you. You are truly His treasured possession, and there will never be another like you.

YOUR WORSHIP IS VALUABLE

The word *bara* in Isaiah 43:7 also means *to carry value,* or in your case, *to be invaluable* simply because God created you and paid the highest price for your redemption. The price tag you carry is the life of the Son of God. This makes you the most expensive item in the universe. "You were bought at a price; therefore glorify God in your body and in your spirit, which are God's" (1 Corinthians 6:20).

Your value to God cannot be fully comprehended or calculated; you truly are His treasure. "We have this treasure in earthen vessels, that the excellence of the power may be of God and not of us" (2 Corinthians 4:7).

We are repositories of His riches, His treasures, His Spirit, and His power. This means that all of God's riches are stored in you. All of His power is in you. All of His Spirit is in you. God has simply filled you with Himself. Your inherent value is the fullness of God living on the inside and your potential value is that His fullness can be released to a needy world through you.

God in His wisdom knew when your value on the earth would be most needed. Your birth and existence is miraculously timed for God to receive your worship and service. He also knew where your value was most needed. He knew where you should live and to whom your value would be most relevant, the people who would need you most. Nothing is a coincidence in God. Your worship to God is valuable to those around you because they are affected by His presence operating in your life.

There are unsaved people waiting to be invited to church. There are sick people waiting for you to lay hands on them for healing. There are drug addicts waiting to be set free, and lonely people desperate for your friendship. God has prepared a harvest of people all around you who are ready to be reaped for the Kingdom. (See John 4:35.) Being a worshiper offers these people the best opportunity for their needs to be met. As they come in contact with true worshipers, they are coming in contact with people who are truly in contact with God.

The Lord desires your worship now, and the world needs your ministry now. You are a blessing to both God and this world. Be bold and walk in that revelation.

Unless you know what you carry, the life you live out on earth may not reflect the full value God has attributed to it. When Mary, the mother of Jesus, was pregnant with Jesus, she was the most valuable person who lived because of whom she carried. She conceived Jesus who is the Word, she carried Jesus the Word, and she birthed Jesus the Word. We are not unlike her since we have been born of the incorruptible seed of God's Word, as 1 Peter 1:23 tells us: "Having been born again, not of corruptible seed but incorruptible, through the word of God which lives and abides forever."

We carry the Word in our hearts by revelation, and we birth the Word by faith. As the Church receives greater revelation of who we carry in these earthen vessels, we will transform the world with His love and power. "To them God willed to make known what are the riches of the glory of this mystery among the Gentiles: which is Christ in you, the hope of glory" (Colossians 1:27).

We need to ask God for a revelation of what we carry. We carry His Word, His Spirit, His power, His wisdom, and His Kingdom. He has great faith in us and will find a generation who will carry out His plan and purpose to fruition before Jesus returns.

Nor will people say, Look! Here [it is]! or, See, [it is] there! For behold, the kingdom of God is within you [in your hearts] and among you [surrounding you] (Luke 17:21 AMP).

God has prepared a harvest of people all around us who are ready to be reaped for the Kingdom.

When you understand who you carry, you will birth the miraculous, just like Mary did.

I will praise You, for I am fearfully and wonderfully made; marvellous are Your works, and that my soul knows very well (Psalm 139:14).

Much use is made of the lifting of hands in praise but there is little understanding of why it is done. The Hebrew word used for praise in Psalm 139:14 is *yadah* and is *an expression of thankfulness with the hands lifted.* It's the way that we praise God for the gift of being alive. The psalmist's praise is in response to the miracle of his existence. Our praise with hands lifted and a confession of thanks on our lips is one of the most powerful expressions. It is an acknowledgement that the Lord who made us has brought us to this privileged place of being able to appreciate His handiwork in us. Next time you lift your hands in praise, thank Him for the fact that you were created. It is a great privilege to be alive.

> When the enemy sees you with your hands raised in praise, it reminds him that his hands no longer hold you captive. Praise God that you have been re-created.

Oh, give thanks to the Lord, for He is good! For His mercy endures forever. Let the redeemed of the Lord say so, whom He has redeemed from the hand of the enemy (Psalm 107:1-2).

The same Hebrew word *yadah* is used in the expression "*Oh, give thanks*" in Psalm 107:1-2. The lifting up of hands with thanksgiving is the way we respond to the joy of being redeemed. God not only wants us to appreciate the fact that we were created but also that we have been re-created.

We don't always have to be conscious of God creating and re-creating us when we lift our hands in praise, but it would be good to remember that it is a scriptural way of responding to Him regarding those two great truths. When the enemy sees you with your hands raised in praise, it reminds him that his hands no longer hold you captive. It's a tremendous expression of freedom.

CHAPTER 2
Delivered to Worship

Nothing should depict the Christian life more than freedom.

You shall know the truth, and the truth shall make you free (John 8:32).

Deliverance means to be set free or rescued from a hostile power that seeks to dominate or enslave. God had deliverance on His mind when He sent Jesus to the world, and Jesus had deliverance on His mind when He came. Jesus was on a mission from the Father to set the captives free; it was His life's work and ultimate goal. Nothing should depict the Christian life more than freedom, yet the lives of so many Christians don't reflect this truth. Scripture says that the truth sets us free.

There is no such thing as freedom without truth. Truth is the air that freedom breathes which enables us to live the super-abundant life God promised. (See John 10:10.) There's a difference between knowledge and truth. Knowledge relates to information, but truth is revelation. We're living in a time when the knowledge of God's Word is available like never before. Knowledge alone, however, can be frustrating because it doesn't set us free—only truth does. Revelation is

God exposing something in His Word previously unknown to us. He has a way of revealing things to us at just the time we need them for a particular situation. Such is the nature of revelation.

Paul urged the church at Ephesus to pray for a spirit of wisdom and revelation in the knowledge of God. "[For I always pray to] the God of our Lord Jesus Christ, the Father of glory, that He may grant you a spirit of wisdom and revelation [of insight into mysteries and secrets] in the [deep and intimate] knowledge of Him" (Ephesians 1:17 AMP).

Ignorance is a chain that enslaves, but truth is the key that opens the door to your freedom. There is no area of your life that needs to be bound in captivity if you are prepared to apply truth to it. His Word has made provision for freedom in every situation you will ever experience.

At the beginning of Jesus' ministry, He spoke these words recorded in Luke 4:18: "The Spirit of the Lord is upon me, because He has anointed me to preach the gospel to the poor; He has sent me to heal the brokenhearted, to proclaim liberty to the captives and recovering of sight to the blind, to set at liberty those who are oppressed."

His anointing was to heal broken, bruised, and sick people. Jesus was a deliverance preacher and freedom was His goal for every man, woman, and child. It's not until we see people delivered that we can say that we are preaching the truth of the Gospel. We need more than good teaching and preaching; we need the anointing to set people free and see them free indeed. As it says in John 8:36, "If the Son shall make you free, you shall be free indeed." And yet, today the Church at large has become so ineffective in this area.

Anything God does is thorough and perfect, including our deliverance. Absolute freedom in every area of our lives is our spiritual heritage to enjoy.

Freedom is the evidence of truth.

You've Been Delivered

Jesus' life and work on earth brought an end to the devil's work and reign over humanity. "For this purpose the Son of God was manifested, that he might destroy the works of the devil" (1 John 3:8).

When Jesus announced on the cross, "*It is finished,*" in John 19:30, it meant He had finished the work of delivering mankind from the controlling power of the devil. From that time until now, all men and women have been given the possibility of temporal and eternal freedom from every work of the devil. There is nothing more God can do to deliver us. His work is finished. Since even the angels, demons, and every spiritual power that exist know that the devil has been defeated because of Jesus, we should embrace Christ's victory and walk confidently in this truth. This truth is confirmed in Colossians 2:15, "Having disarmed principalities and powers, He made a public spectacle of them, triumphing over them in it."

After Jesus had defeated the devil through His atoning work on the cross, He displayed his defeat in a most public way to all spirit beings in the universe. Every angel in Heaven celebrated this astounding victory and every demon shamefully had to acknowledge that satan had been defeated and stripped of all his power over humanity.

> *He stripped all the spiritual tyrants in the universe of their sham authority at the Cross and marched them naked through the streets* (Colossians 2:15 TM).

Jesus stripped the devil of all his power, leaving him with a powerless army. Colossians 2:15 pictures a victorious emperor returning to his people, dragging behind him his captured enemy in chains through the streets. Such public displays took place in ancient times, and the victorious emperor would sing a victory song as he displayed the enemy to his people, who responded with great celebrations. This gives insight into the extent of Jesus' victory and the celebration that should accompany it by believers. Our total deliverance from the work of the devil is something to celebrate every day.

As we exercise this truth by faith in our lives, this reminds the devil and his defeated army that they are powerless over the Church. God has already done everything needed for us to walk in victory over the devil. There is no more work God has to do. Our work is to believe and celebrate, and as we do we will enter into a freedom that we have never before experienced.

He has delivered us from the power of darkness and conveyed us into the kingdom of the Son of His love (Colossians 1:13).

A closer look at the meaning of this Scripture reveals the following: The Greek word for *delivered* is *rhoumai* and means *to rescue*. The delivering power of God that rescued us is far superior to the power that enslaved us. We were delivered from the power, ability, and strength of the devil. If God has delivered us from the power of darkness, then darkness has no more power over us. We are legally free from all activity of the devil because he can only operate in darkness. Darkness is his only geographical influence. We have been removed from it and seated in heavenly places.

> Jesus stripped the devil of all his power, leaving him with a powerless army. We have been rescued from the territorial control of the devil.

YOU'VE BEEN TRANSPLANTED

God spoke to Moses just before He gave him the Ten Commandments. He said: "I am the Lord God, who brought you out of the land of Egypt, out of the house of bondage" (Exodus 20:2).

God told Moses that He had been delivered from two things.

The first is the *land or territory of oppression*. We have been rescued from the territorial control of the devil. In reality, when the devil sees us, he knows he is powerless to hurt us, because we have been delivered beyond his reach, and out of his control. When we take hold of this reality, everything holding us in bondage will be detached from our lives. We have to see ourselves beyond the devil's reach, his influence, and his power. The truth is that he cannot get to us because God has removed us from his control.

> *The devil sees you, but he knows he is powerless to hurt you. You have been delivered beyond his reach and out of his control.*

You have been given a new (covenant) passport stamped with the blood of Jesus. The devil has no access into the Kingdom you live in; he has no passport to enter and no visa. He has been barred from entering the place where you live, the Kingdom of God's dear son. The devil only gains access if you believe his lies. When you do, you provide him with the credentials necessary for entry. He may apply for a temporary visitor's visa, but his plan is to take up permanent residency the moment he crosses the border. And when he does, he'll bring sickness, disease, and poverty with him. Resist his application for a visa, and he will flee.

The second thing God told Moses was that he had been delivered from the *house of bondage*. The word *house* means *family, home, habitation*, and also suggests *intimacy*. We have not only been delivered from the devil's control but also his intimacy. It's true that we were once under his intimate control and manipulation. Our senses and impulses were tuned in to the devil's frequency, and we were *dead* to the things of God. Sin and the nature of the devil were *alive* in us, and in this way we were intimate with the devil and his ways. Colossians 1:21 says: "You, who once were alienated and enemies in your mind by wicked works, yet now He has reconciled."

> *You He has made alive, who were dead in trespasses and sins, in which you once walked according to the course of this world, according to the prince of the power of the air, the spirit that now works in the children of disobedience* (Ephesians 2:1-2).

Things have changed. We now have God as our Father. He wants us to call Him Papa, who loves and cares for us and seeks intimacy with us. The great message Jesus brought us was that God is a loving Father who loves intimacy with His children.

The only way the devil can become intimate with you is when you receive and believe his thoughts. The devil will bombard your mind with thoughts contrary to God's Word. If you don't cast them down, they will become more real to you than God's thoughts contained in the Bible. The devil wants his thoughts to become a way of life for you. He will try to familiarize you with deceptive thoughts, and access a place of intimacy through your thought life. Whenever you cannot get victory in any area of your life, it is most likely because you are still thinking you can't.

We have changed locations, and have a new Father—the Jehovah God. Our previous father (the devil) hated us and hates us still, but our Heavenly Father loves us. So celebrate your freedom.

CELEBRATE YOUR FREEDOM

When the Lord brought back the captivity of Zion, we were like those that dream. Then our mouth was filled with laughter, and our tongue with singing: then said they among the nations, the Lord has done great things for them. The Lord has done great things for us; and we are glad (Psalm 126:1-3).

The Lord turned the captivity of Zion, which is the Church, but notice what accompanied it—laughter and singing. They praised because they appreciated their great deliverance. The Church must be full of praise for what God has done. If we don't appreciate the great deliverance that has already taken place in our lives, how can we believe God for deliverances still to come? Keep praising God for what He has already delivered you from and for what He is yet to deliver you from. God not only wants you to walk in the fullness of deliverance but to be a deliverer of those who are bound.

DELIVERED TO SERVE GOD

One of the first healing incidents in Jesus' ministry was with Peter's mother-in-law, recorded in Mark 1:31: "He came and took her by the hand and lifted her up, and immediately the fever left her. And she served them."

As soon as she was delivered she immediately served. The purpose of deliverance is not just to escape hell and get to Heaven; it is to serve God in this life and throughout eternity. Luke 1:74-75 confirms why we are delivered: "To grant us, that we, being delivered from the hand of our enemies, might serve Him without fear in holiness and righteousness before Him all the days of our life."

122

You are delivered from the hand of your enemy, meaning that he has no hand in your affairs. You are free from his grip. He can't hold on to you in any way, and he cannot stop your service in God's Kingdom as He has planned. God wants you to experience freedom from the work of the devil every day, all the days of your life. None are meant to be days wasted away, full of failure and defeat. This does not mean we won't have challenges and tests, for they help us grow. It means that the devil is not in control of your life even when there are challenges. In Christ every day is a day of freedom and victory. Every day of your life is precious and every day has been created for you to serve God. Serving God is experienced not in what you do for God but in living in the fellowship you have with God through reading His Word, praying, worship, and obedience. This prepares and qualifies us for practical service. Every day of your life has been created to serve the Lord. What a privilege He has given you.

DELIVERED TO WORSHIP

The Greek word for *serve* in Luke 1:74-75 is *latreuo,* meaning *to minister (to God), render, religious homage, to worship.* It has been translated as *one's extreme devotion and service to something he worships with undivided devotion.* God has created us primarily for worship. It is out of this practice that we can serve. A worshiper is the only kind of servant God wants. Life for the Christian is found in these two activities and in that order. It is difficult to consistently serve God unless we consistently worship Him. When we prioritize the worship of God every day, He will find something meaningful for us to do. Effective ministry comes from a worshiping heart.

Bishop David Oyedepo of Nigeria says, "Every frustration in life is related to a lack of worship." Some Christians work hard for God but are still frustrated. This is because they have not developed an intimate, worship-based relationship with Him. God does not want born-again strangers to work for Him. He seeks worshipers with servant's hearts. He has no "correspondence" worshipers. He wants those who have a close and personal, intimate relationship with Him. We are delivered to worship the God who delivered us.

If we find it hard to worship, it would be good to begin by meditating on what God has delivered us from. Our freedom to worship is related to our knowledge and appreciation of deliverance. A free man will appreciate and be thankful to his liberator. Jesus is our liberator who is worthy of endless praise and worship for His redemptive work. The only way to approach God is with gladness, and this should be for our deliverance. When we worship with gladness, the world will see that we have been delivered and will want this deliverance also.

> A free man will appreciate and be thankful to his liberator. Jesus is our liberator.

Serve the Lord with gladness; come before his presence with singing (Psalm 100:2).

The word *gladness* means *with pleasure and joy*. Serving God without joy is not biblical. God only receives our serving when we consider it a pleasure and joy as an expression of our love for Him. No one should serve in God's house without a thankful and joyful heart. Leaders should look for people to serve who love God more than they love the work they are asked to do. Every leader should be a worshiper and worship should be the hallmark of the next generation of leaders.

> *You have turned for me my mourning into dancing; You have put off my sackcloth and have clothed me with gladness, to the end that my glory may sing praise to You, and not be silent. O Lord my God, I will give thanks to You forever* (Psalm 30:11-12).

The result of deliverance is dancing and singing. If we have a revelation of what God has done in our lives, we will sing and dance without restraint. Those who refuse still have not received the revelation of what salvation really means and how they should respond to His saving grace.

> *Vows made to You are binding upon me, O God; I will render praises to You, for You have delivered my soul from death. Have You not kept my feet from falling, that I may walk before God in the light of the living?* (Psalm 56:12-13)

BEWARE OF THE DEVIL'S STRATEGY

There is an interesting passage in Exodus that gives insight into the plan the devil has against worship in the Church. Pharaoh had refused to let Moses and God's people go free, until he was forced through a series of plagues culminating in thick darkness covering the land of Egypt. Then Pharaoh succumbed and ordered Moses to go serve his God. "Pharaoh called to Moses and said, 'Go ye, serve the Lord; only let your flocks and your herds be kept back. Let your little ones also go with you'" (Exodus 10:24).

This sounded good, but there were conditions. He told Moses to leave behind his flocks and his herds. This was highly significant, for the flocks and herds represented two things:

1. They were Israel's means of life support. They could not survive without their animals as a basic food source, and they could not trade without their animals. The animals fed them both naturally and financially.

2. They used the animals to carry out the sacrifices commanded by God. This was their means of worship.

Moses said, you must also give us sacrifices and burnt offerings, that we may sacrifice unto the Lord our God (Exodus 10:25).

Moses said that not one hoof would be left behind or be redundant. Moses was saying that what belonged to him belonged to God, and not even one animal would be considered for anything but God's service.

Our livestock also shall go with us; there shall not a hoof be left behind. For we must take some of them to serve the Lord our God, and even we do not know with what we must serve the Lord until we arrive there (Exodus 10:26).

The devil was content to let Moses go and serve God without the sheep and cattle. What he was intending to do was to allow Moses to serve God, but to remove his ability to worship God with animal sacrifices and financially prosper through his livestock. The same tactics are used by the devil today. He does not mind if we serve in church as long as we don't worship and give of our tithes and offerings. Worship and giving are the two most contested issues in church life today. The devil is still spreading the same lies he did 2,000 years ago, but he has no hope of convincing the present-day Church, as it is liberated from these two strongholds.

The devil's worst nightmare is that you find out the extent of your deliverance and claim it by faith. The only time the devil can influence you is when you give him the right to. He has no more power than you give him. Only you can give him access into your life and only you can remove him from your life. Amazing as these statements may seem, it is true. When we understand that we are totally and absolutely free, it will unleash such an authority and boldness in believers' lives that the world will literally be astounded.

CHAPTER 3

The Power of a Thankful Life

A thankful life is a powerful life.

Telling His Name

In general when someone receives a gift, appreciation is expressed with words like *thank you* or *thanks*. The extent of our thanks is usually in proportion to the value we place on the gift. If we esteem the gift highly, we will usually say "thanks very much" or tell the giver more than once how much we appreciate what we have received.

Some years ago I was teaching a class on thanksgiving and mentioned that in the ancient Hebrew language the word for *thank you* had a different meaning than what is commonly understood today. The emphasis was on declaring or making known the name of the person who gave the gift, or more accurately, "I will declare your name." It was a public acknowledgment of the name of the giver. I had no references to back up my statement, but told the class I did find it interesting.

One of the students in the class was a dentist, and he related an incident that had taken place in Africa years before. He said a poor African man came into his dental rooms with a toothache but had no money to pay for the treatment. The dentist treated him and then told him there would be no charge. The African was insistent on knowing the dentist's full name, thanked him, and left. At the time this made no sense to him, but he had often wondered about it. He asked if there was any correlation with what was being discussed in the class. I didn't know, but in the same class, there was a lecturer in linguistics from one of the country's leading universities. She confirmed that some languages do express thanksgiving by bragging on the name of the giver. She was convinced that this was the poor African's way of saying thanks, and that he would tell others of the good character of the dentist. This incident led me to look more closely at Scripture and see what thanksgiving was about. To my amazement I found confirmation in Scripture of what had been discussed in the class that day.

The Power of a Thankful Heart

One of the greatest privileges in life is to witness to someone about Jesus, but it has to come from a thankful heart. A life that is truly grateful to God for salvation is the most powerful and potent witness for Christ. Young converts are usually effective at witnessing about Jesus. They are thankful for the reality of His presence in their lives that salvation has brought. They value the gift of salvation so highly that they have to tell others about it. This should, in fact, be the case with every believer. Thanking God for salvation should be our priority and lifestyle, and it will be if we esteem salvation as the greatest gift we have received. We read in Ephesians 2:8-9, "By grace you have been saved through faith, and that not of yourselves; it is the gift of God, not of works, lest anyone should boast."

We have received hundreds of testimonies from our School of Worship students around the world, stating that the principles we gave them to develop a lifestyle of thanksgiving revolutionized their lives.

One outstanding testimony came from a young man who had conducted a School of Worship on my behalf. Life was good—he had a wonderful family, led praise and worship in a local church, and was also quite wealthy. But due to adverse circumstances, his wealth evaporated overnight.

He told me how he sat one night with his wife and two small boys and started to weep over his loss. The Lord spoke to him and asked him if he was still saved. He thought it was an unusual thing for the Lord to ask under the circumstances, but he readily replied that he was. The Lord spoke and said to him, "Then you have more than enough to be thankful for."

> A person who is truly grateful to God for salvation is the most powerful and potent witness for Christ.

That moment changed his life. He picked up his guitar and started to give God thanks for his salvation. He knew that God's Word says *in everything* give thanks, rather than *for everything*. He chose to give thanks to God, despite the circumstances. "In everything give thanks, for this is the will of God in Christ Jesus for you" (1 Thessalonians 5:18). This young man's testimony has subsequently helped so many lives.

The distinction between *in everything* and *for everything* is one that many of us fail to make, often because of poor teaching we have received in the past. God does not give us adverse circumstances so we can be thankful, but He might allow adverse circumstances to come our way to see if our thanksgiving is rooted in our salvation. We are not asked to nor should we thank God for sickness or lack in our lives, but we can thank Him that our salvation includes the promise of health and prosperity. (See First John 3:2.)

THE WILL TO THANK

The fact that we are saved does not guarantee a thankful lifestyle, but it does give us the potential to develop one if we are willing. Our will is a God-given faculty and something we have to exercise daily as we are confronted with a plethora of options. Every choice we make has a consequence and will either draw us closer to or lead us further away from God. Scripture makes it clear that thanksgiving is God's will for us; it's His purpose, desire, and pleasure. If thanksgiving were lacking, it would suggest that we are out of the will of God and not in line with His purposes and desires for our lives. However, when we do give thanks in everything, we are aligning our will with His plans for our lives and guaranteeing that our destinies in Him are secure.

> *Every choice we make has a consequence and will either draw us closer to or further away from God.*

WEAVE THANKSGIVING INTO THE FABRIC OF YOUR LIFE

In the restoration of the temple under Ezra, the builders gave thanks when they laid the foundation. (See Ezra 3:10-11.) Any foundation laid without thanksgiving is weak. It doesn't matter how magnificent the building looks. Without the right foundation, it is faulty. At the start of something, whether it's a business, ministry, or relationship, thanksgiving should be woven into the foundation stones. There is wisdom in this practice, in that it helps determine if God is actually in it or not. If it's not something you can give Him thanks for, it's questionable if it was His idea in the first place.

A life devoid of thanksgiving is a life operating at less than full strength. If you are wondering why things are shaky in your life, it might be because your life is lacking thanksgiving. Don't wait another minute. I suggest you put this book down right now and give Him thanks for saving you. This is the first step to strengthening the foundation of your walk with God. Do it daily and you will lay a sturdy foundation for life.

WHAT HAPPENS WHEN WE GIVE THANKS

1. Thanksgiving changes our circumstances.

The prophet Jonah was told by God to go to Nineveh to preach repentance to the people. He was, however, disobedient and tried to flee from the presence of God. On a ship going in the wrong direction, he was thrown overboard and swallowed by a great fish. (See Jonah 1:1-17; 2:1-9.) Although God put him into the fish, he would have died had he done nothing. Cramped inside the belly of the fish with seaweed wrapped around his head and slowly being digested was not the place to be thankful. But Jonah did remember his vows of thanksgiving to God and their association with salvation. He said: "I will sacrifice to You with the voice of thanksgiving; I will pay what I have vowed. Salvation is of the Lord" (Jonah 2:9).

As soon as he gave thanks, God spoke to the fish and commanded it to expel the prophet onto dry land. It's interesting that God spoke to the fish and not the prophet! When Jonah gave thanks to God, he was delivered immediately. God spoke to the fish (representing the circumstances surrounding Jonah) and the fish quickly obeyed. He came from the bottom of the ocean, moved toward dry land, and spewed him out. There was no argument from the fish (circumstance). Everything keeping you bound has to release you when you give thanks.

2. Thanksgiving is the key to unlimited access.

A gate is used for keeping things in and other things out. Thanksgiving seems to be the key that accesses the gate to God's presence. Psalm 100:4 says: "Enter into His gates with thanksgiving, and into His courts with praise. Be thankful to Him, and bless His name."

When you use the key of thanksgiving to open the gate to God's presence, there is nothing that can remain locked to you in this life. God will open doors that no man can shut. (See Revelation 3:8.)

When your life is full of thanksgiving God leaves the door to His presence open, and you are invited to enter anytime, anywhere. Never approach God without thanksgiving in your heart and on your lips.

3. Thanksgiving gets prayers answered.

God allows us to pray so we can fellowship with Him and get our needs and those of others met. The part God loves is the fellowship that prayer enables us to have with Him. The part we love is the answer that prayer brings. This is why Jesus taught His disciples to open their prayers with *Our Father*. This is addressing God in the most intimate way. A revelation of God as our loving Father is the key to addressing God in prayer.

As the Church matures, she will understand and enjoy the fellowship part of prayer more and more. There is no need to rush into prayer with your requests. Take time to approach God worshipfully before you ask for anything, and always close with thanksgiving. Many powerful saints of God know this secret, and get their prayers answered. One great man of God said, "I used to pray long and praise little in my time with God, but now my prayers are shorter and my praise is longer." This man found the secret of enhancing his prayer with thanksgiving.

> There is no need to rush into prayer with your requests. Take time to approach God worshipfully before you ask for anything, and always close your prayer with thanksgiving.

Thanksgiving is the starting point when praying for individuals. If we cannot appreciate them, we are not ready to pray for them. The apostle Paul's prayers started with thanksgiving. Thanksgiving is the launch pad for prayer. It makes prayer reach its target. "We give thanks to God always for you all, making mention of you in our prayers" (1 Thessalonians 1:2).

[I] *do not cease to give thanks for you, making mention of you in my prayers* (Ephesians 1:16).

Timothy suggests that if we pray and give thanks for our leaders, it will affect the peace we experience. Surely the prayers of the saints have a direct effect on the peace and national security of a nation. Paul, the apostle, said: "I exhort first of all that supplications, prayers, intercessions, and giving of thanks be made for all men, for kings and all who are in authority, that we may lead a quiet and peaceable life in all godliness and reverence" (1 Timothy 2:1-2).

When we pray, we are fellowshipping with God by telling Him our needs or the needs of others. When we thank Him, we tell Him that all our needs are met according to His Word.

4. Thanksgiving helps church growth.

Some years ago, I was asked to help a church with their music ministry. It was a good church with a fine pastor who was concerned that his music ministry lacked anointing and acted as a stumbling block to numerical growth. I did my best to re-train the team with sound biblical principles and there was definite improvement. Some years later, I was reminded of that incident. God showed me that with many churches, the problem of church growth is not a lack of outreach or evangelism programs. Instead, it appears to be a lack of thanksgiving within the church. If the saved cannot appreciate salvation within the church, isn't it unreasonable to expect the unsaved to be attracted? It is time to restore the biblical principles of thanksgiving, praise, and worship within the church.

Under the leadership of Nehemiah, at the dedication of the wall of Jerusalem, thanksgiving once again was made a priority. Nehemiah 12:31,40 says: "I brought the leaders of Judah up on the wall, and appointed two large thanksgiving choirs. So the two thanksgiving choirs stood in the house of God, likewise I and the half of the rulers with me."

Two large choirs were specifically assigned to give thanks in God's house. The Scripture says that God had made them rejoice with great joy so that it was heard afar off. (See Nehemiah 12:43.) Their thanksgiving had an effect beyond the walls of the church; it literally extended to distant lands. When the Body of Christ has a *thankful spirit* many will be affected by it outside the walls of the church. It's a spiritual principle that the atmosphere you create within a local church will affect the community—after all, that's why the church exists.

5. Thanksgiving—morning and evening.

Thanksgiving is prioritized in morning devotions. Inviting the presence of God into our day should be the first thing we do in the morning. Equally, inviting His presence into our night should be the last thing we do before we fall asleep. "Stand every morning to thank and praise the Lord, and likewise at evening" (1 Chronicles 23:30).

Thanking God continually may seem like an extreme thing to do but as you develop thanksgiving as a lifestyle, it will seem like the best and most rewarding thing you have ever done.

Jesus Had a Lifestyle of Thanksgiving

Jesus fulfilled the role of God and man while He lived on the earth, and as a man, felt the need to pray, He give thanks, praise, and worship in the same way we do.

1. Thanksgiving has resurrection power.

Jesus was called to come to the tomb of His friend Lazarus, who had been dead for four days. When Jesus arrived, He commanded them to take away the stone from the tomb, and then give thanks to His Heavenly Father for hearing the prayer He had prayed before reaching the tomb. John 11:41-43 says: "They took away the stone from the place where the dead man was lying. And Jesus lifted up His eyes and said, 'Father, I thank You that You have heard Me. And I know that You always hear Me, but because of the people who are standing by I said this, that they may believe that You sent Me.' Now when He had said these things, He cried with a loud voice, 'Lazarus, come forth!'"

In this account, thanksgiving was the public expression Jesus used to let people know God answers prayer. Between the time of the prayer being given and the prayer being answered, there must be thanksgiving. Thanksgiving lets Heaven and hell know you believe what you have prayed. Immediately after Jesus gave thanks, He commanded Lazarus to come forth from the tomb.

The Church is trying to command *dead things* to come to life without thanksgiving. In this instance it was not prayer that sparked the miracle of the resurrection; it was thanksgiving. This doesn't infer that prayer is inferior to thanksgiving, but it suggests that things prayed for come to life when accompanied by thanksgiving. The power released from a thankful heart has the potential to resurrect dead things in your life.

> The power released from a thankful heart has the potential to resurrect dead things in your life.

2. Thank God you live for Him.

One of the last things Jesus did before He went to the cross was have supper with His disciples. The bread was symbolic of Jesus' body and the wine His blood. Matthew 26:26-28 tells us: "As they were eating, Jesus took bread, blessed and broke it, and gave it to the disciples and said, 'Take, eat; this is My body.' Then He took the cup, and gave thanks, and gave it to them, saying, 'Drink from it, all of you. For this is My blood of the new covenant, which is shed for many for the re-mission of sins.'"

Jesus, after taking the cup of wine, gave thanks. He was demonstrat-ing His gratitude for the opportunity to give His life for the remission of sin and the redemption of mankind. He gave thanks that He would be allowed to die so we could live. If Jesus gave thanks for the opportu-nity to die for us, we must give thanks for the opportunity to live for Him now and throughout eternity.

3. Thanksgiving produces multiplied provision.

A large crowd had listened to Jesus preach for three days and were hungry. Jesus took a few loaves and fishes, gave thanks, and told the dis-ciples to feed the multitude. As they proceeded to give the food to the people, it multiplied, for they fed more than 4,000 people. The account in Matthew 15:36 says: "He took the seven loaves and the fish and gave thanks, broke them and gave them to His disciples; and the disciples gave to the multitude."

Jesus gave thanks before He broke the loaves and fishes in anticipa-tion of the miraculous provision that was about to take place. We should not only be thankful for what we have in our hands but also for what can be multiplied through our hands to meet the needs of others.

4. Thank God for revelation knowledge.

On one occasion Jesus gave thanks for things that were hidden and things that were revealed. He was referring to truth contained in God's Word that is hidden from those who intellectualize rather than believe it. Jesus also gave thanks for those who receive God's Word uncompro-misingly and with simplicity. Matthew 11:25 says: "Abruptly Jesus broke into prayer: 'Thank you, Father, Lord of heaven and earth. You've concealed your ways from sophisticates and know-it-alls, but spelled them out clearly to ordinary people. Yes, Father, that's the way you like to work'" (TM).

One of the most important prayers is to ask for the spirit of wis-dom and revelation knowledge. Paul prayed this prayer for the saints at Ephesus with continual thanksgiving: "I also, after I heard of your faith in the Lord Jesus and your love for all the saints, do not cease to give thanks for you, making mention of you in my prayers: that the God of our Lord Jesus Christ, the Father of glory, may give to you the spirit of wisdom and revelation in the knowledge of Him" (Ephesians 1:15-17). Pray this prayer daily with thanksgiving knowing that you can have the wisdom and revelation knowledge of God operating in your life on a continuous basis.

What is interesting in all of the above examples is that when Jesus gave thanks, it produced some kind of miracle. Such is the power of a thankful life.

CHAPTER 4

Praise Changes You

Praise is the outward expression of an inward explosion of God's Word that changes things.

After leading thousands of people in praise and worship every week for years in what many considered an anointed music ministry, I often wondered if there was something missing. I noticed that many people would struggle to worship on a Sunday regardless of how excellent the musicians or anointed the singers. They confessed to loving God, attended church services regularly, and yet it seemed they weren't entering in as completely as they could. If the music ministry could not lift and inspire them, what was the *spark* that would ignite their praise? After months of searching the Scriptures, something became clear that I had not seen before. It was the absence of a catalyst in their lives. This may seem a strange expression to use in relation to praise, but what I discovered made a lot of sense.

THE CATALYST FOR PRAISE

In scientific terms, a catalyst is a substance that increases the rate of a chemical reaction without itself undergoing any permanent chemical change. The significance of a catalyst is that it needs to be present for the reaction to take place.

> Praise is the outward expression of an inward explosion of God's Word.

The born-again experience gives us the opportunity to praise but does not guarantee that we will. Some people who have been saved for many years struggle to actively participate in praise and worship and don't know why. They erroneously believe, or have been incorrectly instructed, that it is because they are not musically inclined or that it's not all that important. But worship is what God seeks. (See John 4:22-23.)

The reason for the struggle is because the catalyst of God's Word is missing. God's Word must be present in our lives for the reaction of praise to take place. Praise is the outward expression of an inward explosion of God's Word. It is the unsolicited release mechanism of our personal revelation of the greatness of God as we have discovered Him in His Word. So if we don't regularly read the Word, we are lacking the essential scriptural context for our praise. Good musicians and great songs certainly help us focus on God, but it is God's Word that ultimately is the praise leader in our hearts. Let's take a look at the following Scriptures that confirm God's Word is the catalyst:

1. It is God's Word that guides the psalmist to the tabernacle to praise Him. Psalm 43:3-4 says: "Oh send out Your light and Your truth! Let them lead me; let them bring me to Your holy hill and to Your tabernacle. Then I will go to the altar of God, to God my exceeding joy; and on the harp I will praise You, O God my God."

2. The psalmist praises God for His Word. If the Word is not present, praise will be absent. Psalm 56:4 says: "In God (I will praise His Word), in God I have put my trust; I will not fear. What can flesh do to me?" Psalm 56:10 confirms this: "In God (I will praise His Word), in the Lord (I will praise His Word)."

3. Praise comes when you learn (know) God's Word. If you don't know God's Word, praise does not come. Psalm 119:7

says: "I will praise You with uprightness of heart, when I learn Your righteous judgments."

4. Rejoicing (praise) comes from God's testimonies (Word). Joy is a fruit of the Spirit that exudes from knowing God through His Word. Psalm 119:14 says: "I have rejoiced in the way of Your testimonies, as much as in all riches."

5. God's Word was the psalmist's song. The source of all Christian singing must be God's Word. If the lyrics don't support biblical truth, the songs do not support praise. Psalm 119:54 says: "Your statues have been my songs in the house of my pilgrimage."

6. The psalmist said he praised seven times a day because of God's Word. We can safely conclude that he was reading or meditating on God's Word seven times a day and that caused him to give praise. He had developed a lifestyle of praise. Psalm 119:164 says: "Seven times a day I praise You, because of Your righteous judgments."

7. The apostle Paul confirmed that praise is the result of God's Word living inside us. Ephesians 3:16 says: "Let the word [spoken by] Christ (the Messiah) have its home [in your hearts and minds] and dwell in you in [all its] richness, as you teach and admonish and train one another in all insight and intelligence and wisdom [in spiritual things, and as you sing] psalms and hymns and spiritual songs, making melody to God with [His] grace in your hearts" (AMP). When God's Word is on the inside, it will come out in psalms, hymns, and spiritual songs.

How Do We Define Praise?

Praise is a person's expression to God either vocally, visibly, or a combination of both in response to the revelation of who He is and what He has done as shown through God's Word. When praise is released from the lips of a believer, it is a spiritual force that lets the principalities and powers know they are defeated, regardless of circumstances. Praise demonstrates the celebration mode we are in because of Christ's victory.

> Faith is a place where mountains of impossibilities are removed and Goliaths lie headless in the dust.

Praise is enforcing God's Word at the highest level and letting everyone know in heaven and earth that you believe it.

THE SUBSTANCE OF PRAISE IS FAITH

Faith is defined as a substance, the substance of things hoped for. Hope is in the future and is something you cannot see except in your mind, but faith gives it substance and brings it into the present. There are three things we need to know about faith that will help us enter into praise.

1. Faith is a spiritual substance that converts your hopes and dreams into realities. Faith takes us into the uncomfortable zone where total reliance for our very existence and success is dependent upon things we don't see in the natural but believe exist because God said they do. It's the place where there is no security in anything except God. Faith is the place where most people would like to live but the residents are few. It is a place where mountains of impossibilities are removed and Goliaths lie headless in the dust. Hebrews 11:1 says: "Now faith is the substance of things hoped for, the evidence of things not seen." In the Amplified Version, it says it this way: "Faith is the proof of things we do not see and the conviction of their reality (faith perceiving as real fact what is not revealed to the senses)."

2. Without faith it is impossible to please God. This being so, it can also be said that faith pleases Him. Nothing we do can ever please God unless it is done by faith. If there is a way to achieve something without God, then faith can often be absent. Conversely, faith is always present if there is dependence on Him. Hebrews 11:6 says: "Without faith it is impossible to please Him, for he who comes to God must

believe that He is, and that He is a rewarder of those who diligently seek Him."

3. Faith comes by hearing over and over. Romans 10:17 says: "Faith comes by hearing, and hearing by the Word of God."

Hearing God's Word over and over by reading, confessing, and hearing it preached, results in something pleasing to God—faith. The starting place in a life that brings pleasure to God is the reading of His Word. It's a wonderful and reassuring thought that every time we read it, God is pleased. And as faith builds through ingesting God's Word, something else is released—praise. For this reason it has been said that praise is the highest expression of faith. It is the fruit from the tree of faith that is rooted in the soil of knowledge.

The Purpose of Praise Is to Change You

God's dream for each one of us is to become more like His Son Jesus. (See Ephesians 4:15.) He is like a doting father who doesn't want to leave his children alone. He continually wants to shape, transform, and mature us and praise is one of the ways He achieves this. Praise brings us face to face with God, expressing our love for what He has done, for what He is doing, and for what He will do for us according to His Word.

All of us, as with unveiled face, [because we] continued to behold [in the Word of God] as in a mirror the glory of the Lord, are constantly being transfigured into His very own image in ever increasing splendour and from one degree of glory to another; [for this comes] from the Lord [Who is] the Spirit (2 Corinthians 3:18 AMP).

Praise is a particularly life-transforming exercise since the Bible tells us that God inhabits the praises of His people. Indeed many of us can testify to the overwhelming sense of His presence in praise. Other translations, such as the New American Standard Bible and the New International Version, convey the idea of God enthroned in the midst of our praises. He is always enthroned whether we praise Him or not. The difference is that when we praise Him, we personally enthrone Him in our lives.

The word *inhabit* in the Hebrew means *to abide* (together, like in a marriage), to sit down and preside with the idea of judgment. Biblical praise is giving God the right to inhabit our lives, much like we share the life of our marriage partner. It allows Him to judge and correct everything that displeases Him so He can achieve His ultimate goal of making us like Jesus. Praise permits Him to transform our lives because we've not only submitted to His Word but expressed (in praise) our absolute faith in it. Psalm 22:3 says: "Thou art Holy, O thou that inhabitest the praises of Israel" (KJV).

Corporate praise is a powerful environment for transformation, but the greatest change happens when praise is developed as a personal lifestyle so that we are transformed one degree at a time. (See Second Corinthians 3:18.)

Through Him, therefore, let us constantly and at all times offer up to God a sacrifice of praise, which is the fruit of lips that thankfully acknowledge and confess and glorify His name (Hebrews 13:15 AMP).

THE MOTIVATION FOR PRAISE IS LOVE

The motivation for God to change us is His deep, endless love for us. Praise must be personal and from the heart to our best friend, Jesus. If our praise is based on anything outside of a personal love relationship with Him, it is not true praise but a substitute. Jesus made this principle clear when He spoke to the Pharisees, who searched the Scriptures for truth but would not come to the One who was Truth. (See John 5:39-40.) They refused an intimate relationship with the Person of Truth. Sadly, we see a similar thing happening today—Christians who want to keep Jesus at a safe distance when it comes to loving Him. Proverbs 8:17 says: "I love those who love Me, and those who seek Me diligently will find Me." If we keep Jesus at a distance, He will remain there. When we embrace Him, He will embrace us.

Galatians 5:6 tells us that faith works by love. Praise must also work by love, because as explained above, it is the highest expression of faith. A love for God is what makes our praise real. If we do not have love, we will lack faith and certainly won't be able to praise. Love is above all things, and it has no competitors. It is impossible for love to fail. When we praise God from a foundation of love, nothing can stop our praise from moving mountains. Everything submits to love. Nothing can withstand its presence, because God is love. Love is the most permanent and everlasting power in the universe, and it abides forever. (See First Corinthians 13:13.) Because love is above all things, all things bow in its presence.

When we praise, we must be motivated by one thing only, and that is love. We praise because we love God so much. Praising God is our expression of love for Him from a heart of faith. I suspect that our praise might have a permanent record in Heaven.

CHAPTER 5

The Worshiping You

When God finds the worshiping you, He has found what He is looking for.

WORSHIP IS IMPORTANT TO GOD

God seeks worshipers. The meaning of the word seeking is to search out in order to find, to crave or demand something from someone. It gives the strong impression that whatever is being sought is of utmost importance to the seeker and is prioritized above everything else.

If we grasp the truth of this, we see that God literally craves our worship, not because He needs it, but because we need to give it. There must be something so powerfully beneficial for us when we worship that it would cause the Father to seek it the way He does in our lives. What a profound privilege it is to satisfy the desire of God's heart when we worship.

When God finds the *worshiping you,* He has found what He is looking for in you. Everything else you do is of secondary importance and a consequence of worship. This is a core truth of this amazing subject and a challenge the Church must embrace. How long will we continue to labor so diligently for God, only to accept results that in our hearts we know fall short of what God desires? If we are to see greater Kingdom results, we must be prepared to accommodate a paradigm shift that sees worship *in spirit and in truth* throughout the Church at large.

WORSHIP IS THE ATMOSPHERE OF GOD'S PRESENCE

While as born-again believers we have God's abiding presence in our lives, the realization of this fact varies with each individual. To some God is an intimate, loving Father, but to others He seems far away. While God makes Himself available without reserve to all believers, not everyone avails himself or herself of His presence.

God is not a respecter of persons, but He is a respecter of seekers. He is drawn to those who seek Him. If we put God at a distance, He will stay there, but if we embrace Him, He will run to us, as did the father of the prodigal son. God's desire is for intimacy. He already knows each individual intimately, and He wants us to reciprocate this by getting to know Him intimately too.

God's goal is for us to experience His presence in everything we do. Moses, in fact, said that there was no use going anywhere without God's presence.

> *Moses said, "If your presence doesn't take the lead here, call this trip off right now. How else will it be known that you're with me in this, with me and your people? Are you travelling with us or not? How else will we know that we're special, I and your people, among all other people on this planet Earth?"* (Exodus 33:15-16 TM)

The cry of men and women's hearts that love God is "without Your presence, let's call it off!" Many are tired of programs, events, conferences, worship, teaching and preaching that are devoid of Him. The desperate hunger for God Himself to be powerfully present in church is growing and nothing less will satisfy, nothing of value will work or be sustained without Him.

It was once said that "religion is all that remains when God has left the room." Just because we have a church meeting doesn't mean we have a meeting with God. If God is not present in our meetings, there is no reason to have them. But when He is present, the unchurched will find a reason and a purpose for being in our meetings. God is their only hope, and He must be found in our churches.

The unchurched are looking for the supernatural, and we must offer them a God who is evident in our midst with the power to heal, deliver, set free, and comfort. The unchurched are looking for tangible evidence of God in the lives of Christians. They want more than mere words; they want evidence that our lifestyle is different from theirs. These folks visit our churches because they want a better life and know in their hearts that God can help them. The last thing they are looking for is people who are no different from themselves and a church that is empty of God's presence and power.

> *All the multitude kept silent and listened to Barnabas and Paul declaring how many miracles and wonders God had worked through them among the Gentiles* (Acts 15:12).

While many good church programs are successfully attracting the unchurched, the greatest testimony is that they are coming and staying because they feel and experience God's presence. The presence of God and worship can never be separated; where worship is given, His presence will be found. It is necessary for sustainable revival. When the revival meetings are over and the evangelists have all gone home, the lifestyle of worship we have adopted will perpetuate His manifest presence and power. Continuous revival should be the experience of every true worshiper because of his or her continual intimacy with God and obedience to Him. God's plan is for nothing less. James 4:8 says: "Draw near to God and He will draw near to you. Cleanse your hands, you sinners; and purify your hearts, you double-minded."

The onus is on each individual to determine the level of personal revival he or she wants and take the necessary steps to gain it, sustain it, and grow it. It's all about intimacy and obedience and there is no limit.

Our inheritance is to dwell in His presence, the greatest privilege He has given us. We see in Psalm 140:13: "Surely the righteous shall give thanks to Your name; the upright shall dwell in Your presence."

This is a picture of the overcoming, triumphant believer and of the glorious end-time Church. It is an exciting time for the Church as she calls out to God for nothing more or less than to experience Him. Worship is the spiritual atmosphere we need to exist; without it we are out of breath and gasping for spiritual sustenance. The Church of today is hungry for His continual presence.

How Do We Define Worship?

Defining worship is a challenging task because it encompasses every aspect of the life of the believer. However, the Hebrew and Greek words used in the testaments have a common meaning—*being in close proximity to God when in the act of worship.*

The most commonly used Hebrew word for worship is *shachah*, and from this root, we have the meaning of *a pit or well, a deep cistern, a place where we can go lower down or sink into.* Worshipers in the Old Testament demonstrated worship by prostration, bowing down, falling on their knees with their foreheads touching the ground in reverence. They had a simple response to God's presence requiring little action, noise, or demonstration.

In the New Testament, the Greek word commonly referring to worship is *proskuneo,* formed from the prefix *pros,* which means *in front of someone* or *in the direction of someone,* and the verb *kuneo,* which means *to kiss.* This word has the same root as *shachah* and has been defined as *prostration, falling down to one's knees to worship, adore, revere, to move toward or in front of with the intention to kiss.* New Testament worship does involve movement and intimacy.

Putting these ideas together, we can conclude that worship is a movement (a step of obedient faith) toward God with the intention of intimacy. This is not in terms of spatial movement, however, for God does not come down from Heaven nor do we go up to Heaven when we worship Him. Heaven is a place that exists in a different dimension and is instantly accessible when we worship. It's like a door that opens when we worship rather than a journey we take.

In John 4:23, Jesus said that true worshipers will worship the Father in spirit and truth. Worship is now in the present, meaning that your access to God's heart and everything it has to offer is possible anytime you choose. God, who has already made His move to live in our hearts, allows Himself to live through us as we worship. Wherever He is, His kingdom exists and manifests through our lives in accordance with His Word and His Spirit. Luke 17:21 says: "Indeed, the Kingdom of God is within you."

God's Kingdom is a spiritual kingdom that resides within us when we are born again and operates through us when we allow Christ to reign as King in our lives. Worship is the expression of our gratitude to the King, His Kingdom, and our obedience to serve in it.

WORSHIP IS WORTHSHIP

A derivative of the word worship is the word *worthship* meaning *an acknowledgement of worth or value.* Worship is essentially the response we have to the value or appraisal (importance, preciousness, estimation, price) we attribute to God. The degree to which we value God will be reflected in our worship.

Lucifer was created to worship and serve God, and yet he led a rebellion in Heaven, convincing one-third of the angels to follow him. Lucifer's problem was rooted in pride, which caused him to overestimate his own worth and importance while devaluing God. He progressively moved away from worshiping God to worshiping himself, valuing his own worth as greater than God's, which ultimately lead to outright anarchy and rejection of God.

God has made Himself known to all men (see Rom. 1:19-20), but even those who have accepted Him as Lord don't value and subsequently worship Him equally. The value (worth-ship) we assign to God is expressed by the extent to which we worship and obey Him. The more we get to know Him, the more we will value Him and the more we will give Him unrelenting worship.

WORSHIP IS INTIMACY

Just as faith is in the present tense, so is worship. Remember what we read in Hebrews 11:1? "Now faith is the substance of things hoped for, the evidence of things not seen."

The time for worship is *now.* The Father is seeking your worship right now in the present continuous tense, not just on Sundays or when you meet with other believers. Corporate worship should be an overflow of the personal, intimate worship we give God on a continuous basis throughout the week. It's difficult to be intimate with God in public if you are not intimate with Him privately. As we develop a lifestyle of worship through a continual consciousness of God, our worship on Sunday (or whenever we go to church) will be an overflow of it. The worship team's function is not to stir us up to worship but to facilitate the overflow.

Worship is so uncomplicated; it's letting God know how much you love Him in your own personal way. He is your Dad, the one person who loves you at all times and wants you to visit Him any time, day or night—He's always ready. Although it might help, music isn't necessary for worship. All you need is an intimate relationship.

Worship is a continual state of being conscious of an awesome, powerful, loving God who is ever ready to heal, deliver, and set us free from every work of the devil. When God occupies our thoughts, worship will continually flow from our hearts and lips. Developing a continual consciousness of God keeps us in the spirit realm of His presence. When we worship we are connected to God's realm, and when we develop a lifestyle of worship, we keep ourselves connected. Worship is so practical. It is allowing God to be a decision-maker in all that we do and a witness in all that we say. It's welcoming Him into every aspect of our lives, personal and public. Someone used the expression, "worship is up close and personal," and it is. David understood it when he said in Psalm 16:8: "I have set the Lord always before me; because He is at my right hand I shall not be moved."

David did not want God to leave him at any time. David knew he needed to take action on a repeated basis (a lifestyle) to make this happen. He *set the Lord before him,* meaning that he would not allow God to be out of his thoughts or actions. Worship is the inclusion of God in everything in our lives.

WORSHIP IS OBEDIENCE

The subject of worship is understood by many as the singing of slow songs as an act of adoration. There is no doubt that this is an expression of worship, but worship is much more than merely singing songs. It is about obeying God. Scripture says that obedience is better than sacrifice. God loves to hear us sing, but He loves it more when we obey. "Has the Lord as great delight in burnt offerings and sacrifice, as in obeying the voice of the Lord? Behold, to obey is better than sacrifice" (1 Samuel 15:22). We also read in Hosea 6:6: "I desire mercy and not sacrifice, and the knowledge of God more than burnt offerings."

The first time the word *worship* is used is when God asked Abraham to come up to Mount Moriah and sacrifice his son Isaac as an act of worship. (See Genesis 22:2.) It was a giant step of faith and one of the greatest acts of obedience in the Old Testament. It foreshadowed a lifetime of absolute obedience by Jesus to His Father that enabled Him to get to Calvary.

I wondered why we are told in the Gospels that Jesus gave thanks, praised, and rejoiced, but there is no reference that says He worshiped. It could be God wants us to understand that worship is more than expressing our love through music. It is expressing our love through obedience. Jesus' life of absolute obedience to the Father God epitomized worship. It was a life of obedience that enabled Him to die on the cross for all humanity. One act of disobedience by Jesus to the will of His Father would have disqualified Him. Worship is ultimately measured by obedience. Could it be that the depth of our worship is better gauged by our response to the last thing He told us to do? I wonder if this is more of a test than how lovingly we sang our last song to Him?

More than once, God has asked my wife and I to move from one continent to another. On one occasion, I felt reluctant because I had built up quite a ministry profile in the nation. This is the message He spoke to my heart: "Tom, you can stay here and be comfortable and still operate in your anointing, but I will be in another place waiting for you." I immediately got in touch with the Department of Immigration to find out how to make the move. I learned one valuable lesson. The greatest place of your anointing is in the place of obedience, because it's where God is waiting for you.

> Could it be that the depth of our worship is better gauged by our response to the last thing He told us to do? I wonder if this is more of a test than how lovingly we sang our last song to Him?

No matter how musically accomplished it might be, praise and worship from a disobedient heart cannot compare to the words sung or spoken from a heart of obedience. This is the worship He seeks. The greatest measure of worship is obedience to His written Word and personal instructions for your life. Obedience is the place where God is glorified the most. (See John 17:4.)

Psalm 47 sums up who God is and why we should value and worship Him above all else.

> *The Lord Most High is awesome;*
> *He is a great King over all the earth....*
> *Sing praises to God, sing praises!*
> *Sing praises to our King, sing praises!*
> *For God is the King of all the earth;*
> *Sing praises with understanding.*
> *God reigns over the nations;*
> *God sits on His holy throne.*

WORSHIP ENTHRONES GOD

Scripture tells us that God inhabits (is enthroned) in the praises of His people. A throne is associated with *rulership*—power and authority. God is always on the throne and has ultimate power and authority whether we praise or worship Him or not. The significance, however, is that when we worship Him, we enthrone Him in our lives and circumstances, and His power is released to dethrone everything contrary to His will for us. This is why the devil hates worship and will do everything he can to hinder us from doing it. He doesn't want to be dislodged from influencing our lives.

Worship in the local church is also very important for the same reason. When God is enthroned in corporate worship, the effect is devastating against the corporate seat of iniquity the devil has set up in that geographical area. Jesus told the Samaritan woman that worship was not subject to geography, but that geography was subject to worship. John 4:20-23 says: "Our fathers worshiped on this mountain, and you Jews say that in Jerusalem is the place where one ought to worship." Jesus said to her, "Woman, believe Me, the hour is coming when you will neither on this mountain, nor in Jerusalem, worship the Father."

This means that ruling spiritual forces in geographical areas are subject to the worship of that area. If the devil is worshiped, demonic powers remain but if God is worshiped, they are removed. Worship changes things in the spirit realm that significantly affect things in the natural realm for both individuals and churches. The victory over the enemy is decisively the Lord's, but the devil will continue throughout the Church age to lure God's people away from worship and strengthen his position of authority and influence over them.

The worshiping Church is emerging and removing ungodly thrones and establishing godly ones in geographic areas where local churches and home groups meet to worship.

CHAPTER 6
Children Born in Zion

A generation born in Zion (the Church), raised by God-fearing parents, have a special and prophetic place in the end-time Church.

A generation of young people born in Zion (the Church) and raised by God-fearing parents have a special place in the end-time Church. At every level of growth in children, God has made provision for them to be nurtured in His presence. In these troubled times, when the divorce rate in many nations, even among Christians, is as much as fifty percent, when single parents are an accepted norm, and the traditional family unit is fast becoming an extinct species, it is important to address the issue of God's place in the Christian home.

There are a few questions we should ask ourselves. Are the biblical principles we so willingly say amen to on Sunday practiced in our homes? Do Christian children honor their parents? Are we praising fathers and joyful mothers at home? Is the home a place of prayer and praise? Is the home a place of joy and peace? If we can't say amen to these questions, we must ask ourselves why.

THE RESPONSIBILITY OF PARENTS

Often the greatest joys and greatest heartaches in our lives stem from our role as parents. God's Word tells us that children are a blessing from God (see Psalm 127:3), and we know this to be true. And yet, there are times when we wonder if it really has to be as difficult as it seems. Many aspects of today's modern culture add to the challenge of effective parenting, gnawing away at the confidence and authority God has assigned to us as Christian parents. (See Proverbs 22:6.)

One consequence of this is that we can succumb to these pressures and fail to fulfill the responsibilities God's Word has set down for us. Ephesians 6:4 instructs us: "Bring [your children] up in the training and admonition of the Lord." If we neglect this responsibility, and fail to effectively model appropriate God–honoring lives before our children, we shouldn't be too surprised if they show little interest in making Jesus the Lord of their lives. Though we may hope that children's church will do a good job with Bible readings and God-focused activities, it is the home where the greatest testimony of God's existence should be.

One beautiful little boy in our church recently came up and stared at me for a few seconds before his mother reached me and said, "Pastor Tom, he thinks you are God." I told him that was *not* true, but I could see he wasn't convinced. To him I was God walking around the church. I later thought about the incident and realized how much influence pastors have on their congregants. In the same way, parents have influence on their children and must be diligent to serve as godly role models. It's wonderful for children to read about Jesus in the Bible, but a far greater impact is made when young people see their parents demonstrating godly characteristics.

So much emphasis has been placed on winning the world for Jesus, and we must do so, but our efforts should not be at the expense of the Christian home. If we cannot win our children to Jesus, there is little merit in leaving the house to evangelize the world. God has a great plan for Christian families in the last days, and He has promised to do a magnificent work by pouring out His Spirit on our sons and daughters. Acts 2:17 promises: "It shall come to pass in the last days, says God, that I will pour out of My Spirit on all flesh; your sons and your daughters shall prophesy...."

There is arising a generation of children and young people mentored by godly parents who will have a special place in the end-time move of God. They are children who are born in Zion (the Church), raised by God-fearing parents, and they carry a strong calling on their lives. It starts with choosing the right marriage partner.

THE SEED OF GODLY PARENTS

Scripture tells us not to be unequally yoked, meaning that we shouldn't marry anyone who is not a believer. (See Second Corinthians 6:14.) One of the reasons for this is the potential of children growing up in an environment of spiritual conflict. Although some spiritually mixed marriages may work, they are not God's best for a couple or their children. Mixed spiritual seed can produce conflict regardless of well-intentioned plans. God's plan is for children born in Zion (the Church) to be raised by God-fearing parents who nurture and raise their children in the things of God.

NURSING INFANTS

Even at a young age we see that God has a wonderful promise for nursing babies. Psalm 22:9 says: "You are He who took me out of the womb: You made me trust when I was upon my mother's breasts."

The Amplified Bible says it this way: "You made me hope and trust when I was on my mother's breast." The word *trust* means to be safe, confident, and to feel assured and secure. This psalm was prophetically referring to Jesus, but the promise applies to every nursing mother who trusts in the Lord. Even before the child gains cognizance of the world around it, God gives it a sense of security through a believing mother.

Scripture also clearly associates joy with motherhood. Psalm 133:9 says: "He grants the barren woman a home, like a joyful mother of children. Praise the Lord!" And there is Proverbs 23:25: "Let your father and your mother be glad, and let her who bore you rejoice."

Children bring much joy, but joy comes from trusting God's Word. Jeremiah says that it was God's Word that gave him joy. "Your words were found, and I ate them, and Your Word was to me the joy and rejoicing of my heart; for I am called by Your name, O Lord God of hosts" (Jeremiah 15:16).

The instruction from the angel who visited Mary announcing that she would give birth to Jesus was to be joyful. She immediately rejoiced and started to magnify the Lord with song. (See Luke 1:46-55.) God wanted Jesus brought up in an atmosphere of faith and joy in His Word. This is God's prescription for the baby as well as the mother, especially in a day when postnatal depression is on the increase and children are growing up with insecurity and fear.

A nursing mother who is a worshiper gives her child such a tremendous beginning in life, transferring her faith and joy in the Lord to her child. A joyful home will strengthen and prepare our children for life more than we can imagine.

The principle is that anything God births should bring joy. As the things He has birthed in us grow, we need to maintain faith and joy in His Word. If we fail to be joyful, we risk losing our strength while bringing those things to maturity. Scripture says in Nehemiah 8:19: "The joy of the Lord is your strength." Everything seems to thrive and grow strong in an atmosphere of joy.

THE HOME IS A PLACE OF WORSHIP

The Old Testament patriarchs such as Abraham, Isaac, and Jacob built altars and took responsibility to lead their families in times of worship to God. Passover was an annual observation of Israel's deliverance from Egypt, and Scripture shows us that God wanted it to be celebrated in the home, ensuring that the tradition would be handed down through the generations. (See Exodus 12:1-4.) Passover is a classic example of God's dealings with the nation at a family level. He wants His presence known and celebrated in the home. The family home should be the most influential place for children to learn of God's character and His Word.

Matthew 5:15 says: "Nor do they light a lamp and put it under a basket, but on a lampstand, and it gives light to all who are in the house." This Scripture is referring to our witness in general to the world, but the reference to the word house is dwelling place or abode—the place where we live.

Christianity must shine bright in our homes and our spouses and children must be the recipients of the fruit of God's transforming power in our lives. Home is a challenging place for all of us because it's the environment where our character is constantly tested through relationships with those closest to us. If we don't pass the test in the home, it is doubtful God can use us outside of its walls. As an individual, I don't have to ask anyone how well I am doing in representing Christ and His Kingdom. I just have to ask my wife or children. The pulpit is second to the home when it comes to ministry. When the home reaps the first fruits of our character in Christ, we qualify and are equipped to impact the world.

GOD'S PRESENCE IN OUR HOMES

A wonderful example is when God's presence resided in Obed-Edom's house for some months. The Philistines captured the ark of the Lord, which carried God's presence. It was held for some time before King David reclaimed it and brought it back to Jerusalem. David angered God, however, because he used men who were not ordained of God to carry the ark. In his confusion, David decided to leave the ark in the house of a man called Obed-Edom until he better understood how God wanted it to be transported.

> *David would not move the ark of the Lord with him into the City of David; but David took it aside into the house of Obed-Edom the Gittite. The ark of the Lord remained in the house of Obed-Edom the Gittite three months. And the Lord blessed Obed-Edom and all his household* (2 Samuel 6:10-11).

The Lord not only blessed Obed–Edom but also his family. Because the father obviously had respect for the presence of God, the blessing was extended to everyone in the home. Respect for the presence of God still brings blessings upon a home and the family that lives there. If there is no father in the house or he is not saved, the blessing can still come through the mother.

The word *blessed* in this Scripture means *to benefit abundantly or greatly*. God's presence was in the home of Obed-Edom and his family for three months, and they benefited greatly. It is hard to imagine the effect it would have had on him and his family, even on his neighbors. God had come home, and by default, Obed-Edom and his family got the blessing. How much more blessing will we get by prioritizing God's presence in our homes.

JESUS' PRESENCE IN OUR HOME

Zacchaeus was a tax collector who heard that Jesus was passing through town. The streets were lined with people taking up a position to see Him, but because Zacchaeus was short, he had to leave the crowd behind, run ahead, and climb a tree in order to see Jesus. If you want to see Jesus, you have to leave the crowd behind and make a special effort. Climbing the tree was not the kind of thing one would expect a rich tax collector to do, but his desire to see Jesus was greater than his pride. They might have mocked him when he went up the tree, but they must have been amazed when Jesus stopped and asked Zacchaeus to come down because He wanted to stay at his house that night. Luke 19:5 gives the account: "When Jesus came to the place, He looked up and saw him, and said to him, 'Zacchaeus, make haste and come down, for today I must stay at your house.'"

Jesus was so impacted by Zacchaeus' effort to see Him that He put His plans on hold. When we go out of our way to see Jesus, He will literally stop what He is doing to visit us. Zacchaeus' family would never be the same after that visit. The tax collector's wife and children would never forget the day they hosted the Son of God because of their father's determination. Nothing has changed, Jesus is still found in the homes of those who are extravagant in their pursuit of Him.

CHILDREN

Jesus made it very clear that the children should come to Him. (See Mark 10:13-16; Luke 18:15-17.) He took them up in His arms and blessed them. In Matthew 21:15-16, there is evidence that some children not only believed in Jesus but also worshiped Him. From these Scriptures it is clear that Jesus expects the very young to know and praise Him. As parents of young children, we must take up the responsibility to encourage them to trust and praise the Lord. In Psalm 145:4, the simple instruction on how to do this is provided for us: "One generation shall praise your works to another, and shall declare your mighty acts."

Parents should be praising God for the works (miraculous things) He has done for them as a testimony to their children. As children hear the testimony of God's faithfulness to their parents, they will believe in Him also. As this is modeled by parents, we can expect to see a generation of young children in these end times whose praise will stop demonic activity in its tracks and astound the world. Psalm 8 declares: "Out of the mouth of babes and infants, You have ordained strength, because of your enemies, that you may silence the enemy and the avenger."

YOUTH

Teenagers born in Zion will be mightily used in the Church because they honor God, their parents, and those in godly authority. Exodus 20:12 says: "Honor your father and your mother, that your days may be long upon the land which the Lord your God is giving you." We read it again in Ephesians 6:2-3: "Honor your father and mother, which is the first commandment with promise: that it may be well with you and you may live long on the earth."

The word honor means to revere, respect, to put a value to. The value young people ascribe to their parents is important—so important that their lives may depend on it.

This is a sobering message in light of the all-out assault on the honor of parents we are seeing today. Godly wisdom will be required to ensure that the Church avoids the negative impact of this. As it says in 2 Timothy 3:1-2: "In the last days perilous times will come: For men will be lovers of themselves, lovers of money, boasters, proud, blasphemers, disobedient to parents, unthankful, unholy."

In the end times, one of the characteristics of low morals is disobedience to parents. God, however, reminds us later in the same chapter (2 Timothy 3:15-17) that His Word is an antidote for children who rebel. When they are taught the Scriptures from a young age, they grow up valuing and implementing God's Word, whether it is to convict them of sin or to help them correct their mistakes. When children obey and respect God's Word, it is natural for them to obey and respect their parents. This is the generation that is now arising in the earth. These young people love God and are securing the wonderful promises of God that go along with honoring parents, one of which is long life.

YOUTH USED BY GOD

There is a misconception that God cannot use young men and women to lead the Church in many areas of ministry. It may be true that they may lack a degree of wisdom and experience, but God responds to people who have faith regardless of their ages. God used some teenagers in the Bible in a most remarkable way.

The apostle Paul encouraged young Timothy not to be intimidated because of his youth but to be an example to others. (See 1 Timothy 4:12.)

YOUTH WHO BIRTH THE MIRACULOUS

Mary, for example, was no more than 15 or 16 years old when she gave birth to Jesus. Her great faith at such a young age was demonstrated when she declared that the birth of Jesus should be in accordance with the Word of God she had just received from the angel of the Lord. "Mary said, behold the handmaiden of the Lord; be it unto me according to thy word" (Luke 1:37).

Under the circumstances, it was impossible for this young virgin to fall pregnant. But this remarkable young woman exercised her faith and lifted her heart and voice in praise to God. Luke 1:46-47 says: "Mary said: 'My soul magnifies the Lord, and my spirit has rejoiced in God my Savior.'"

Young people are becoming spiritually pregnant with the things of God. They are literally full of God's presence, just as Mary was, and they are birthing the miraculous in God's Kingdom.

YOUTH WHO LOVE GOD'S HOUSE

Joshua is referred to as a young man who loved God's presence so much that he would not leave the tabernacle. "His servant Joshua the son of Nun, a young man, did not depart from the tabernacle" (Exodus 33:11).

God's presence was more important to him than people. He did not seek fellowship with man over fellowship with God. Just as in Joshua's day the tabernacle was a place of worship and prayer, the local church must be a place of God's presence, a place of faith, a place of worship, and a place of prayer for our young people. These are the ingredients we need to attract and build a younger generation that is able to stand firm in their faith and take ground for the Lord.

While it's important to encourage healthy social interaction with dynamic youth groups and activities, these alone will not equip our youth to cross the Jordan. God wants young people to cross over and secure the promises the last generation was unable to secure. The promised land awaits occupation by a young generation—those who are bold and courageous way beyond what has been seen or heard before.

YOUTH WHO ARE PROPHETIC

The Scriptures make it clear that the Spirit of God will be poured out upon all flesh in the last days. One of the evidences of this will be prophecy. "It shall come to pass in the last days, says God, that I will pour out of My Spirit on all flesh; your sons and your daughters shall prophesy, your young men shall see visions, your old men shall dream dreams" (Acts 2:17).

Although the outpouring is for everyone, it is interesting that the Scripture first makes reference to young people (sons and daughters) who will prophesy.

The messages we hear from pulpits across the nations are filled with prophetic content. Our songs of praise are prophesying His return and bringing a greater awareness of the soon return of the Lord. Even the secular media has sensed the impending changes that are about to take place in the world and filled movies and magazines with prophetic doom. They are becoming aware of God's prophetic timetable, even if they do not recognize it as such.

The prophetic mantle will operate in the lives of young people who are determined to hear His voice. The music ministry will play a vital role in conveying His prophetic message to their generation.

YOUTH WITH KINGDOM AUTHORITY

The word *Judah* means *praise* and the word *sceptre* is associated with *authority or rulership*. In the Amplified Version, Genesis 49:10 says:

"The sceptre or leadership shall not depart from Judah, nor the ruler's staff from between his feet, until Shiloh [the Messiah, the Peaceful One] comes to Whom it belongs, and to Him shall be the obedience of the people."

David was a young man who expressed his love for God's Word through praise while looking after his father's sheep. When King Saul rejected God's Word and the prophet Samuel was grieving over the incident, God reassured him that He had made provision for someone to take the throne of Israel. "The Lord said to Samuel, How long will you mourn for Saul, seeing I have rejected him from reigning over Israel? Fill your horn with oil, and go; I am sending you to Jesse the Bethlehemite. For I have provided Myself a king among his sons" (1 Samuel 16:1).

God described David the young shepherd boy as a king. David was qualified to rule Israel because he understood covenant authority and worshiped God accordingly. In the sheep fields, the open sky was his tabernacle of praise and the place where Kingdom authority was birthed in him. David made references to God's creation in many of his psalms. He would no doubt have gazed into the night sky and seen the awesome majesty of God's creation in the heavens, watched God paint colorful canvases every morning and night as the sun rose and set, and praised and worshiped Him in response. Psalm 78:70-71 says: "He chose David, his servant, handpicked him from his work in the sheep pens. One day he was caring for the ewes and their lambs, the next day God had him shepherding Jacob" (TM).

God is still looking for worshipers who love His Word. He is earmarking this young generation with Kingdom authority, because He has found them in the *sheep fields* of His presence. They are mighty and fearless, and we have not seen anything like them before in Church history. Ungodly giants might be mocking them now, but only because they have no idea where these young people have spent their time and in whose presence they have been. All Heaven will be released through them and every giant will lie headless in the dust.

What a day to be young and what opportunities await those who are in love with God and His Word. There's never been a better time than the present for young people to take their authority and astound the world with His presence and power.

> There's never been a better time for young people than the present to take their place and astound the world with His presence and power.

CHAPTER 7
Influence of Worship on Healing

Since you are created to worship, it's only reasonable to assume that it must have a healthy effect on you.

God has not only saved us but also wants us to enjoy everything that salvation provides for us, including good health. We read in 1 Timothy 6:17, "Command those who are rich in this present age not to be haughty, nor to trust in uncertain riches but in the living God, who gives us richly all things to enjoy."

The Greek word for *enjoy* in this Scripture means *to get the best out of what belongs to you.* The word for *enjoy* in the Hebrew means *to take full possession and benefit from your inheritance* (God's Word) *by driving out the previous or illegal tenants.*

All of us at some stage are attacked with sickness, but we must resist it with faith in the knowledge of God's Word and in the power of the Holy Spirit to heal us. Perhaps the most important key to fighting sickness is to be absolutely convinced that God is neither the source of sickness nor the perpetrator of it. (See James 1:17 and Psalm 145:9.) God is the source of healing and health, life and vitality.

ENJOY GOD'S QUALITY OF LIFE

The source of sickness (physical, mental, and emotional) and disease is unquestionably the fall of man and the entrance of sin into the world. (See Romans 5:12.) The devil's nature is to kill, steal, and destroy and sickness is one of the primary tools he uses to accomplish this. The nature of Jesus, however, is far superior to his. Jesus came to give us abundant life and is eager and willing to heal us. John 10:10 says: "The thief does not come except to steal, and to kill, and to destroy. I have come that they may have life, and that they may have it more abundantly."

The Greek word for *life* is *zoe,* which means *the absolute fullness of life belonging to Him.* God continually and unreservedly offers us the quality of life that He experiences, free from demonic influence, sickness, and depression. All He asks is that we appropriate His promises by faith. (See Psalm 91:16 and Proverbs 3:1-2.) It almost sounds too good to be true, but this has been accomplished by Jesus at Calvary and agreed upon by the Godhead after Calvary. We read in Acts 10:38, "God anointed Jesus of Nazareth with the Holy Spirit and with power, who went about doing good and healing all who were oppressed by the devil, for God was with Him."

WORSHIP IS AN ENVIRONMENT OF HEALING

Apart from the vast evidence of healings that have occurred during praise and worship in both evangelistic crusades and local church meetings, Scripture affirms that worship opens up a pathway for healing to occur. We see this when King Saul is distressed by a spirit of infirmity. (See First Samuel 16:14-23.) Rather than call for the services of a counselor or physician, his servants recommended that a musician be called to play so that the king could recover. Saul's servants knew the power of worship to affect healing and deliverance, so they sought out young David, a mighty man of valor, who was close to God and skillful in playing the harp. This man after God's heart, the greatest worshiper in the Old Testament, played worship to His God in King Saul's presence. In the midst of this worship, the demon of infirmity harassing Saul departed.

In Isaiah 61:3, we are told to put on the garment of praise for the spirit of heaviness. "To console those who mourn in Zion, to give them beauty for ashes, the oil of joy for mourning, the garment of praise for the spirit of heaviness; that they may be called trees of righteousness, the planting of the Lord, that He may be glorified." The Amplified Bible says "the garment [expressive] of praise instead of a heavy, burdened, and failing spirit."

In these instances references are made to sickness in connection with demonic activity. It seems that praise is an atmosphere where demons of infirmity feel most uncomfortable and leave. Could it be that there is nothing more powerful we can do in order to receive our healing than to praise when the symptoms of sickness start pulling us down? Let the lifestyle of praise and worship keep demonic activity away from you.

EXPECT HEALING WHEN YOU WORSHIP

We again see the influence of worship in the life of the leper who was healed. "Behold, a leper came and worshiped Him, saying, 'Lord, if You are willing, You can make me clean.' Then Jesus put out His hand and touched him, saying, 'I am willing; be cleansed.' Immediately his leprosy was cleansed" (Matthew 8:2-3).

People almost certainly ran in horror as he approached, but his desire for healing was greater than any fear of rejection or ridicule he might have felt. You may have to be bold publicly in your demonstration of worship to receive your healing.

The leper began to worship Jesus, knowing only that He could heal him. He wasn't certain if Jesus was willing. But Jesus reached out and touched him as he worshiped, and he was immediately cleansed. This man's act of worship revealed the heart of Jesus. It confirmed that He is willing to heal us. When we worship we move the hand of God to heal us.

The Bible says the leper was healed *immediately*, meaning instantaneously, without delay. And since God healed this man instantly in the act of worship, why wouldn't He do it for you in your act of worship? If you are sick or recovering from sickness, establish a routine of worship to God in your schedule, even if for just a few minutes a day. Expect healing to take place during your worship. Use this Scripture as a reference to receive your healing as you worship. God's ability and willingness is just as powerful today—all that is required is worship and the expectation of healing.

Worship seems to draw the manifestation of healing forward in time so that it occurs while worship is being offered to God. People should always be encouraged to receive healing during times of private and corporate worship.

Don't Ever Give Up—Sickness Is Not Your Heritage

In Matthew 15:22-28, we find a Canaanite woman who begged Jesus for mercy for her daughter who was possessed by demons. She fell down in worship to Him and cried out for help. Jesus told her that He was sent to preach to the lost sheep of the house of Israel, but she would not give up. She said she would be content with the crumbs left over from what He offered the Jews. What she was implying was that, although she might be considered a dog (a non-Jew), her act of worship proved that Jesus was her Master. Through this act of worship and the exercise of her faith, she was in a position to receive the crumbs (God's Word) from her Master's table. Jesus commended her great faith, and her daughter was immediately healed.

Since Jesus has come for everyone who believes in His name, we can expect to sit at the Master's table and eat the food He provides, regardless of our nationality, culture, race, or language. Worship gives us that right and privilege.

You Cannot Afford to Neglect Worship
When You Are Sick

Sickness at its ultimate is death. The ruler had just lost his daughter (see Matthew 9:18-19; 23-26), and yet when he approached Jesus, he worshiped Him. It is amazing to think that this man could offer worship in the midst of such circumstances. Yet, he remained certain that Jesus could raise his daughter from the dead—so certain that he could worship. The life of Jesus was greater in his sight than the death of his daughter. He worshiped the one who was Life, and then asked Jesus to come and impart life again to his little girl. Jesus followed him home, took the girl's hand, and she arose. There is great strength in a man known to be a worshiper. Certainly for this little girl, reaching out to and worshiping Jesus was the most important thing her father had ever done. Her life-long testimony would have been that her father was a worshiper. Worship focuses on life while sickness focuses on death. We have to choose one or the other. You cannot afford to neglect worship when you are sick. There's too much to lose, and so much to gain (healing).

Worship is a spiritual force that creates an atmosphere where God is enthroned and circumstances and demonic powers are dethroned. There is no power in hell that can stand in that environment. In the days to come, some of the greatest manifestations of healing the Church will experience will be in times of worship.

> In the days to come, some of the greatest manifestations of healing the Church will experience will be in times of worship.

GOD'S WORD IS THE KEY TO HEALING

The New Testament physician Luke tells us Jesus taught His followers that the power of God was present to heal. "It happened on a certain day, as He was teaching, that there were Pharisees and teachers of the law sitting by, who had come out of every town of Galilee, Judea, and Jerusalem. And the power of the Lord was present to heal them" (Luke 5:17).

In Psalm 107:20, God's Word says: "He sent His Word and healed them and delivered them from their destructions."

The power of God to heal is contained in His Word. Proverbs 4:20-22 says: "My son, attend to my words; consent and submit to my sayings. Let them not depart from your sight; keep them in the center of your heart. For they are life to those who find them, healing and health to all their flesh."

In the Message Bible, verse 22 says: "Those who discover these words live, really live; body and soul, they're bursting with health."

Praise is the highest expression of faith because we celebrate what God said in spite of the circumstances that try to contradict His truth. Because God said "by whose [Jesus] stripes you were healed," healing exists for you. It's not hope; it's a reality. God's promises exist in the spirit realm and are brought into the natural realm by faith. Listen to what 1 Peter 2:24 has to say: "Who Himself bore our sins in His own body on the tree, that we, having died to sins, might live for righteousness—by whose stripes you were healed."

We know that your healing is a very personal issue with God because He said *you were healed*. You may not have the manifestation of healing in your body, but it already exists for you to receive. Healing exists because God said it and it's personally for you now. Be encouraged in times of sickness to release the dynamic power of faith by using His healing Scriptures to praise Him and receive your healing. The Bible is alive and powerful and sharper than any two-edged sword. Hebrews 4:12 tells us: "The Word that God speaks is alive and full of power [making it active, operative, energizing, and effective]; it is sharper than any two-edged sword, penetrating to the dividing line of the [a]breath of life (soul) and [the immortal] spirit, and of joints and marrow [of the deepest parts of our nature], exposing and sifting and analyzing and judging the very thoughts and purposes of the heart" (AMP).

God has spoken His Word, but when you speak it into your circumstances, you make it a two-edged sword. Your spoken agreement with the Great Physician's Word directs it like a scalpel into the inner recesses of your body, cutting out what is not of God and bringing health and restoration.

JOYFULNESS

We are commanded to be joyful (see Deuteronomy 28:47-48;60-61), and failure to do so opens up the doors for every kind of disease. Negativity, worry, and anxiety not only affect us emotionally and mentally but over time affect our health. In Psalm 51, David is repenting before God and asking God to help him be joyful. He knows the combination of repentance and joy will positively affect his health.

Nehemiah 8:10 declares, "The joy of the Lord is your strength." It is the defense by which we can expect to be physically sound and healthy.

Our attitude and general demeanor has a profound effect on our health. In Proverbs 17:22, we are told: "A merry heart does good, like medicine, but a broken spirit dries the bones."

Merry in Hebrew is *sameach,* meaning *glad, joyful, rejoice, cheer up. Medicine* means *to cure, to remove as a bandage from a wound.* A heart that is rejoicing in God will help to keep us in a good state of health.

The Bible commentator Adam Clarke said, "Nothing has such a direct tendency to ruin health and waste our life as grief, anxiety, fretfulness, bad tempers, etc. All these work death."

Joyfulness is a good indicator of health, so *joy* your way to healing and enjoy good health.

CHAPTER 8
Worship Releases God's Kingdom

Surely God's plan is that every believer is a worshiper and every church a worshiping church.

The Church is undergoing a tremendous transition and many have been saying we are in a significant time in Church history—a time when the emphasis is on the King and His Kingdom.

The purpose of the Church is to manifest the Kingdom on earth and worship is a major part of that process. There is a prophetic call to the Church to prepare for the coming King. For this to happen, there must be an understanding and practice of biblical worship. The King of Kings will return for a worshiping Kingdom and a worshiping Church. Surely God's plan is that every believer is a worshiper and every church a worshiping church. When the Church worships, the King is enthroned in our lives and circumstances, taking the Church into supernatural realms of God's works and ways. It's not enough that we operate in His works with miraculous power, miracles, signs, and wonders. We must also operate in His ways with the wisdom of God to positively change society.

GOD'S KINGDOM

God's purpose is for the manifestation of His Kingdom on earth. Jesus had one message: the Kingdom. In Luke 4:43, He says: "I must preach the kingdom of God to the other cities also, because for this purpose I have been sent."

He came to earth to establish His Kingdom; there was no other reason. "This gospel of the Kingdom will be preached in all the world as a witness to all the nations, and then the end will come" (Matthew 24:14).

The Kingdom message has to be preached before Jesus returns to earth. The prophetic timetable for the Church is dependent on the Kingdom message, but what is that message? God's Kingdom is His will, His plans and purposes for humanity to give us an abundant life free from fear, sickness, poverty, and oppression, right here on earth. It's about a Kingdom of priests who exhibit godly character and a Kingdom of kings who exercise godly authority. Revelation 1:6 says: "To Him who loved us and washed us from our sins in His own blood, and has made us kings and priests to His God and Father, to Him be glory and dominion forever and ever. Amen."

The King has also appointed His citizens to expand His Kingdom by operating as kings and priests. By so doing, we synchronize God's plans and purposes for this world with Heaven's timetable.

Jesus is returning for a Church whose character and power are a witness to the world. As a born-again believer, His Kingdom is in you. "Nor will they say, 'See here!' or 'See there!' For indeed, the Kingdom of God is within you" (Luke 17:21).

The reason you exist is to release the Kingdom; and yet, there is no guarantee that the Kingdom is released through you just because you are born again. You may be a carrier, but not a supplier of the Kingdom, and this is where worship becomes vital.

WORSHIP RELEASES THE KINGDOM

When Jesus taught the disciples how to pray, He gave a remarkable insight into the Kingdom. He said: "In this manner, therefore, pray: Our Father in heaven, Hallowed be Your name. Your kingdom come. Your will be done on earth as it is in heaven" (Matthew 6:8-10).

God's name is *hallowed,* which means the worshiper *sets it apart from all other names as holy.* It is an expression of worship, reverence, and godly fear. The next part of the prayer is for the *Kingdom to come,* which means *to find a place of influence in the life of the worshiper.* It appears that those who hallow (worship) God are candidates for the Kingdom to be released through them, influencing not only themselves but those around them. As we worship our Father in Heaven, His Kingdom is released on earth.

Hebrews 12:28-29 says: "Since we are receiving a Kingdom which cannot be shaken, let us have grace, by which we may serve [worship] God acceptably with reverence and godly fear. For our God is a consuming fire."

The Greek word for *serve* also means to *worship.* We need grace to grasp the revelation that God's Kingdom dwells within us and that thanksgiving and worship are the first steps to releasing it. Our primary responsibility is to serve God with worship in reverence and godly fear and then let service flow from it. The Message interprets Hebrews 12:28-29 this way: "Do you see what we've got? An unshakable kingdom! And do you see how thankful we must be? Not only thankful, but brimming with worship, deeply reverent before God. For God is not an indifferent bystander. He's actively cleaning house, torching all that needs to burn, and He won't quit until it's all cleansed. God himself is Fire!"

We are reminded in the Scripture that God is a consuming fire. He will not tolerate Kingdom activity from those who don't hallow and reverence Him with godly fear.

KINGDOM WORSHIP

Kingdom worship is our appreciation of the King and His Kingdom. It is a state of continual thanksgiving, praise, and worship based on the revelation we have of the nature of the King and the greatness of His kingdom.

The enemy of Kingdom worship is anything that takes our priority away from getting to know God better, thinking continuously about Him, serving Him, or giving of our resources to Him. Kingdom worship is simply being sold out to the King and His Kingdom in every area of our lives. It's His invisible Kingdom becoming more real to us than the physical kingdom in which we live. It's when we are more aware of Him than ourselves, His plans rather than our own, His Kingdom rather than ours. Kingdom worship is not an act of worship but a Kingdom mentality, a lifestyle.

KINGDOM LEADERSHIP

A danger to Kingdom worship is the worship of man, especially of those in positions of authority in the church. Whenever church leadership exercises control over someone, they position themselves as illegitimate kings in God's Kingdom.

There is only one King in the Church and only one who is worthy of praise. Although it is right to honor our leaders, we have to remember that there is a fine line between honor and worship. God is raising up leaders who have no interest in controlling His people. These leaders will be Kingdom-focused. They will exemplify Kingdom living to their congregations, disciple them in Kingdom principle, and lead them to seek and worship the King in spirit and truth. In doing so, they will find the greatest honor and reward.

Contact the Author

Tom Inglis

Sydney Life Church / Psalmody International

P.O. Box 224

Mosman, NSW, 2088 Australia

www.psalmody.org

www.sydneylifechurch.com

Ministry Resources

School of Worship

God's purpose for humanity is to know Him intimately. Out of that flows service to Him and a life that is meaningful. If our understanding of worship is lacking, it will affect our quality of life and our perception of why we are living. Only when we understand our purpose can we order our lives accordingly.

The School of Worship will help you get your priorities in line with God's purpose for your life through the understanding and development of a lifestyle of worship. Worship is interwoven into every aspect of living in the Bible including healing, warfare, prosperity, prayer, evangelism, and church growth, to name a few. The three levels of study explore these subjects and many more.

Level 1—Foundation Principles of Worship

You will learn the purpose of life and the foundation principles of worship that will transform your walk with God. Level One is designed to put things in order in your life and to transform your thinking and actions. You will not only understand the importance of intimacy with God, but you will also better understand your authority as a Kingdom citizen.

Three Levels of Study

Each level consists of 13 lessons of progressive study, taught by Tom Inglis on DVD, and includes a Facilitator DVD Starter Pack (13 lessons on DVD, student manual, and workbook). Participation is free for students with the option

to purchase a Student Pack (including manual, workbook, and certificate upon course completion). Any group— large or small—such as Bible schools, connect groups, worship teams, or mid-week church meetings can implement the courses by purchasing the Facilitator Pack.

To start a School of Worship or study as an individual, go to www.psalmody.org or send an email to: contact@psalmody.org.

CHILDREN'S COURSES

Psalmody for Children

Harry Halal in praise

Psalmody for Children is a unique course of lessons designed to equip children's church teachers to teach children how to develop a lifestyle of worship.

The story is based on a couple called Mr. and Mrs. Judah, who were promised by God that they would have a large family. For years they believed, but nothing happened. Eventually they understood that God wanted them to adopt orphans and street children. Over a period of time, they take seven children into their home from different backgrounds and cultures. Each child is given the name and personality of one of the seven major Hebrew praise words. The course covers many biblical principles including, but not limited to, salvation, healing, not being fearful, and praise. The course is suitable for:

1. Children's church / Sunday school classes

2. Children's private school Scripture classes

3. Homeschooling or home instruction by parents

The Program Overview

There are 12 chapters, with four lessons per chapter, suitable for four age groups (2-5; 6-8; 9-10 and 11-13), plus review lessons. The program is designed as a one-year course. A story is woven throughout each chapter, and the lessons progress to a deeper level of understanding as the age groups get older.

Each lesson includes a discussion time, activity, and activity sheet. Each activity sheet is different and varied from the last lesson.

Teachers are encouraged to incorporate some of their own activities, such as games, songs, etc.

You do not have to be a professional teacher to facilitate these lessons. The teacher's manual is easy and simple to use with added reference notes for the teachers to increase their knowledge and stimulate their own study of the Word.

Sammy

Our vision is to teach our children to know God intimately and prepare them for a lifetime of serving Him.

Shabach with Dog and Children Playing

Additional copies of this book and other book
titles from DESTINY IMAGE™ EUROPE
are available at your local bookstore.

We are adding new titles every month!

To view our complete catalog online, visit us at:
www.eurodestinyimage.com

Send a request for a catalog to:

Via Acquacorrente, 6
65123 - Pescara - ITALY
Tel. +39 085 4716623 - Fax +39 085 9431270

"Changing the world, one book at a time."

Are you an author?

Do you have a "today" God-given message?

CONTACT US

We will be happy to review your manuscript
for the possibility of publication:

publisher@eurodestinyimage.com
http://www.eurodestinyimage.com/pages/AuthorsAppForm.htm